Henri Bo

The Printed Book

Henri Bouchot

The Printed Book

1st Edition | ISBN: 978-3-75233-950-5

Place of Publication: Frankfurt am Main, Germany

Year of Publication: 2020

Outlook Verlag GmbH, Germany.

THE PRINTED BOOK

BY

HENRI BOUCHOT

PREFACE.

ONSIDERING that this short study can claim to be nothing more than a rapid and somewhat summary survey of the history of THE BOOK, it eschews all controversial matter, nor does it pretend to convey much fresh information to those already possessing a special knowledge of the subject. It is rather a condensed, but at the same time, it may be hoped, a useful, compendium of the thousand unknown or now forgotten essays, involving endless contradictory statements, that have been issued on this theme. The mere enumeration of such works would simply suffice to fill a volume. We have accordingly no intention to attempt a bibliography, satisfying ourselves with the modest avowal of having found so many documents in all languages, that the very abundance has been at least as embarrassing to us as the lack of materials may have been to others.

The Book appealing in its present form to a special public interested more in artistic than in purely typographical topics, our attention has been more particularly given to the illustrators, the designers, engravers, etchers, and so forth. Such graphic embellishment seemed to us of more weight than the manufacture of the paper, the type-casting, the printing properly so called. This technical aspect of the subject has been very briefly dealt with in a separate chapter, and has also been enlarged upon in the early section. To the binding also we have devoted only a single chapter, while fully conscious that a whole volume would not have sufficed merely to treat the subject superficially.

At the same time, we would not have the reader conclude from all this that our book abounds in omissions, or has overlooked any important features. The broad lines, we trust, have been adhered to, while each section has been so handled as to give a fair idea of the epoch it deals with. This is the first attempt to comprise within such narrow limits an art and an industry with a life of over four centuries, essaying to describe its beginnings and its history down to our days, without omitting a glance at the allied arts.

The engravings selected for illustration have, as far as possible, been taken from unedited materials, and have been directly reproduced by mechanical processes, while fifteen new illustrations, having special relation to the history of the Book in England, have been added to this edition, which is also considerably enlarged in the text on the same subject.

CHAPTER I.

14 . . TO 1462.

Origin of the Book—Engravers in relief—The St. Christopher of 1423—Origin of the Xylographs—The Xylographs, *Donatus*, and *Speculum*—The Laurent Coster legend—From block books to movable characters—John Gaensefleisch, called Gutenberg—The Strasbourg trial—Gutenberg at Mayence—Fust and Schoeffer—The letters of indulgence—The Bible—The Catholicon—The Mayence Bible—Causes of the dispersion of the first Mayence printers—General considerations.

LIKE its forerunner, Painting, the Book has ever been the most faithful reflection of the times when it was written and illustrated. Natural and genuine from the first, and simply embellished with crude illustrations, it assumed in the sixteenth century the grand airs of the Renaissance, gay or serious according to circumstances, decked in what were then called *histoires*—that is to say, wonderful engravings—and daintily printed in Gothic, Roman, or choice Italic characters. But at the close of the century it had already abandoned *wood* for line engravings, heightening its mysticism or its satire at the whim of passing politics and religious wranglings. Then, under the influence of the painters and courtiers of the *Grand Monarque*, it becomes completely transformed, donning the peruke, so to speak, indulging in allegory and conventionalities, pompous and showy, tricking itself out in columns and pilasters instead of the old arabesques and scroll work of the Renaissance, thus continuing amid the coquetries of the regency, the pastorals and insipidities of the following reigns, until at last it suddenly assumes with the heroes of the Revolution the austere mien and airs of classic art. The Book has always been as closely connected with the manners of our predecessors as art itself. The artist submits more than he thinks to the tendency of his surroundings; and if he at times makes his taste appreciated, it is because he has more or less received his first influence from others.

In the sixteenth century the fashion of emblematic representation placed under the portrait of Gaston de Foix a figure of a young plant in full bloom; and the inscription in Latin was "Nascendo maturus"—"Mature at birth." The Book deserves the same device; from its first day up to now it is a marvel of simplicity and harmony. The tentative efforts which preceded the discovery of printing were but few; it may be said that from the moment that Gutenberg conceived the idea of separating the characters, of arranging the words in the forme, of inking them, and of taking a proof on paper, the Book was perfect.

At best we see in following times some modifications of detail; the art of printing was mature, mature from its birth.

But before arriving at the movable type placed side by side, and forming phrases, which appears to us to-day so simple and so ordinary, many years passed. It is certain that long before Gutenberg a means was found of cutting wood and metal in relief and reproducing by application the image traced. Signs-manual and seals were a kind of printing, inasmuch as the relief of their engraving is impressed upon a sheet by the hand. But between this simple statement and the uncritical histories of certain special writers, attributing the invention of engraving to the fourteenth century, there is all the distance of legendary history. Remembering that the numerous guilds of *tailleurs d'images*, or sculptors in relief, had in the Middle Ages the specialty of carving ivories and of placing effigies on tombs, it can be admitted without much difficulty, that these people one day found a means of multiplying the sketches of a figure often asked for, by modelling its contour in relief on ivory or wood, and afterwards taking a reproduction on paper or parchment by means of pressure. When and where was this discovery produced? We cannot possibly say; but it is certain that playing cards were produced by this means, and that from the year 1423 popular figures were cut in wood, as we know from the St. Christopher of that date belonging to Lord Spencer.

It is not our task to discuss this question at length, nor to decide if at first these reliefs were obtained on wood or metal. It is a recognised fact that the single sheet with a printed figure preceded the xylographic book in which text and illustration were cut in the same block. This process did not appear much before the second quarter of the fifteenth century, and it was employed principally for popular works which were then the universal taste. The engraving also was nothing more than a kind of imposition palmed off as a manuscript; the vignettes were often covered with brilliant colours and gold, and the whole sold as of the best quality.

The first attempts at these little figures in relief discovered by the image-makers and diffused by the makers of playing cards were but indifferent. The drawing and the cutting were equally unskilful, as may be seen in the facsimiles given by M. H. Delaborde in his *Histoire de la Gravure*. An attempt had been made to put some text at the foot of the St. Christopher of 1423, and the idea of giving more importance to the text was to the advantage of the booksellers. At the mercy of the writers who fleeced them, obliged to recoup themselves by the exaggerated prices of the most ordinary books, they hoped to turn engraving to account in order to obtain on better terms the technical work needed for their trade. At the epoch of the St. Christopher, in 1423, several works were in vogue in the universities, the schools, and with the public. Among the first of these was the Latin Syntax of Ælius Donatus on the eight parts of speech, a kind of grammar for the use of young students, as well as the famous *Speculum*, a collection of precepts addressed to the faithful, which were copied and recopied without satisfying the demand.

Fig. 1.—Part of a *Donatus* taken from a xylograph, the original of which is preserved in the Bibliothèque Nationale.

To find a means of multiplying these treatises at little cost was a fortune to the inventor. It is to be supposed that many artisans of the time attempted it; and without doubt it was the booksellers themselves, mostly mere dealers, who were tempted to the adventure by the sculptors and wood-cutters. But none had yet been so bold as to cut in relief a series of blocks with engravings and text to compose a complete work. That point was reached very quickly when some legend was engraved at the foot of a vignette, and it may be thought that the *Donatus* was the most ancient of books so obtained among the "Incunabuli," as we now call them, a word that signifies origin or cradle.

The first books then were formed of sheets of paper or parchment, laboriously printed from xylographic blocks, that is to say wooden blocks on which a *tailleur d'images* had left in relief the designs and the letters of the text. He had thus to trace his characters in reverse, so that they could be reproduced as written; he had to avoid faults, because a phrase once done, well or ill, lasted. It was doubtless this difficulty of correction that gave the idea of movable types. If the cutter seriously erred, it was necessary to cancel altogether the faulty block. This at least explains the legend of Laurent Coster, of Haarlem, who, according to Hadrian Junius, his compatriot, discovered by accident the secret of separate types while playing with his children. And if the legend of which we speak contains the least truth, it must be found in the sense above indicated, that is in the correction of faults, rather than in the innocent game of a merchant of Haarlem. However, we shall have occasion to return to the subject of these remarks. It should be well established that engraving in relief on wood alone gave the idea of making xylographic blocks and of composing books. Movable type, the capital point of printing, the pivot of the art of the Book, developed itself little by little, according to needs, when there was occasion to correct an erroneous inscription; but, in any case, its origin is unknown. Doubtless to vary the text, means were found to replace entire phrases by other phrases, preserving the original figures; and thus the light dawned upon these craftsmen, occupied in the manufacture and sale of their books.

According to Hadrian Junius, Laurent Janszoon Coster (the latter name signifying "the discoverer") published one of the celebrated series of works under the general title of *Speculum* which was then so popular (the mystic style exercising so great an attraction on the people of the fifteenth century), the *Speculum Humanæ Salvationis*. Written before the middle of the fifteenth century, made popular by manuscripts, in spite of its fantastic Latinity and of its false quantities, this ascetic and crude poem was easy of access to the xylographists. Junius, as we see, attributes to Laurent Coster the first impression of the *Speculum*, no longer the purely xylographic impression of the *Donatus* from an engraved block, but that of the more advanced manner in movable types. In point of fact, this book had at least four editions, similar in engravings and body of letters, but of different text. It must then be admitted that the fount was dispersed, and typography discovered, because the same cast of letters could not be adapted to different languages. On the other hand, the vignettes do not change, indicating sufficiently the mobility of the types. In comparison to what may be seen in later works, the illustrations of the *Speculum* are by no means bad; they have the appearance, at once naïve and picturesque, of the works of Van Eyck, and not at all of the style of the German miniaturists; properly illuminated and gilded, they lent themselves to the illusion of being confounded with the *histoyres*, drawn by the hand, and this is what the publisher probably sought.

All the xylographic works of the fifteenth century may be classed in two categories: the xylographs, rightly so called, or the block books, such as the *Donatus*, and the books with movable types, like the *Speculum*, of which we speak. This mystic and simple literature of pious works for the use of people of modest resources found in printing the means of more rapid reproduction. Then appeared the *Biblia Pauperum*, one of the most celebrated and the most often reproduced, and the *Ars Moriendi*, a kind of dialogue between an angel and a devil at the bedside of a dying person, which, inspired no doubt by older manuscripts, retained for a long time in successive editions the first tradition of its designs. On labels displayed among the figures are found inscribed the dialogue of the demons and angels seeking to attach to themselves the departing soul, the temptations of Satan on the subject of faith, and the responses of the angel on the same subject.

We can see what developments this theme could lend to the mysticism of the fifteenth century. Composed in eleven designs, the *Ars Moriendi* ran up to eight different editions. From the middle to the end of the fifteenth century, the text was in Latin, then in French, under the title *L'Art au Morier*. In the French edition will be found the blocks that served for the second impression of the work. About 1480, more than fifty years after the first essays, the *Ars Moriendi* enjoyed so much vogue that it employed all the resources of typography as much as in its earliest days. The original subjects, copied in a very mediocre manner, adorned the text, which was composed in Gothic letters, with a new and more explicit title: *Tractatus brevis ac valde utilis de Arte et Scientia bene moriendi* (4to, s.l.n.d.), but the order is inverted, figure 5 of the xylograph becoming No. 3 of the edition of 1480.

Fig. 2.—Xylographic figure from the *Ars Moriendi*, copied in reverse in the *Art au Morier*.

The *ArsMemorandi*, another xylographic work, of which the subject, taken from the New Testament, was equally well adapted to the imagination of the artists, had also a glorious destiny. The work originally comprised thirty blocks, the fifteen blocks of text facing the fifteen engravings. The designs represented the attributes of each of the Evangelists, with allegories and explanatory legends. Thus, in that which relates to the Apostle Matthew,

No. 1 represents the birth and genealogy of Jesus Christ,

No. 2 the offerings of the Magi,

No. 3 the baptism of St. John,

No. 4 the Temptation of Christ,

No. 5 the Sermon on the Mount,

No. 6 the parable of the birds.

The angel that supports the whole is the emblem of St. Matthew the Evangelist.

This mnemonic treatment of the Gospels began with symbols of which we have no means of finding the origin, but which without doubt were employed many centuries earlier. However that may be, their success was as great as that of the already-quoted works. In 1505 a German publisher put forth an imitation, under the title of *Rationarium Evangelistarum*; and this time the copier of the illustrations, retaining the tradition of the first xylographers, no less reveals an artist of the first order, at least a pupil of Martin Schongauer. Some of the conceptions of the *Rationarium* recall exactly the engravings of the great German master, among others that of the Infant Jesus (plate 12), which nearly approaches the style of the Infant Jesus of Schongauer; besides, the principal figures leave but little doubt on the subject. The same wings are on the angels and on the eagles, the same coiffures on the human characters, often the same attitudes.

Fig. 3.—Figure of the school of Martin Schongauer, taken from the *Rationarium Evangelistarum* of 1505, and copied from the corresponding plate of the *Ars Memorandi*.

From the preceding can be judged the extraordinary favour these productions enjoyed. From their origin they were diffused through the whole of Europe, and attracted the attention of excellent artists. Nevertheless their beginnings were difficult. The movable types used, cut separately in wood, were not constituted to give an ideal impression. We can understand the cost that the execution of these characters must have occasioned, made as they were one by one without the possibility of ever making them perfectly uniform. Progress was to substitute for this irregular process types that were similar, identical, easily produced, and used for a long time without breaking. Following on the essays of Laurent Coster, continuous researches bore on this point; but as the invention was said to be his, and it being of importance to him not to divulge it, so that he should not lose his profit, much time was lost over it in his workshop without much success. Here history is somewhat confused. Hadrian Junius positively accuses one of Laurent Coster's workmen of having stolen the secrets of his master and taken flight to Mayence, where he afterwards founded a printing office. According to Junius, the metal type was the discovery of the Dutchman, and the name of the thief was John. Who was this John? Was it John Gaensefleisch, called Gutenberg, or possibly John Fust? But it is not at all apparent that Gutenberg, a gentleman of Mayence, exiled from his country, was ever in the service of the Dutch inventor. As to Fust, we believe his only intervention in the association of printers of Mayence was as a money-lender, from which may be comprehended the unlikelihood of his having been with Coster, the more so as we find Gutenberg retired to Strasbourg, where he pursued his researches. There he was, as it were, out of his sphere, a ruined noble whose great knowledge was bent entirely on invention. Doubtless, like many others, he may have had in his hands one of the printed works of Laurent Coster, and conceived the idea of appropriating the infant process. In 1439 he was associated with two artisans of the city of Strasbourg, ostensibly in the fabrication of mirrors, which may be otherwise understood as printing of *Speculums*, the Latin word signifying the same thing. These men needed to surround themselves with precautions; printing was as yet only a practical means of multiplying manuscripts, to impose a little on the innocent, and fortune awaited him who, without saying anything, made this invention serve him. The following will prove this, as well as its tendency.

A legal document discovered in 1760 by Wencker and Schoepflin in the Pfennigthurm of Strasbourg, and afterwards translated into French by M. Leon de Laborde, makes us at length acquainted with the work of Gutenberg and of his associates Andrew Dritzehen and Andrew Heilmann. Apparently these three men were, as we have said, *Spiegelmacher*, that is makers of mirrors. They had jointly entered into a deed by the terms of which, if one of the partners died in the course of their researches, his heirs would have no rights beyond an indemnity corresponding to the amount invested by him. It happened that Andrew Dritzehen did die, and that one of his brothers aspired to occupy his place in the partnership. The dead man left debts behind him; he had squandered his florins by hundreds in his experiments. Gutenberg having offered to pay the amounts expended, the heirs of Dritzehen, who wanted more, summoned him before the courts to show why he should not make place for them in the work of experiments and making of mirrors. The witnesses in their testimony before the court told what they knew of the inventions of the partnership. One among them deposed that after the death of Dritzehen, Gutenberg's servant went to the workshop and begged Nicholas Dritzehen, brother of the deceased, to displace and break up four formes placed in a press. A second testified that the works of Andrew had cost him at the least three hundred florins, an enormous sum for those days. Other witnesses painted Gutenberg in a curious light: they made him out to be a savage, a hermit, who concealed from his associates certain arts of which the deed stipulated nothing. One fact proved that the experiments referred to the manufacture of metallic characters. A goldsmith, named Dünne, maintained that he had received more than a hundred florins for printing material "das zu dem trucken gehoret." "Trucken!"—"Typography!" The word was found, and from that day usage has consecrated it.

Before 1439, then, John Gaensefleisch, or Gutenberg, was devoted to the art of reproduction of texts, and had consecrated his life and feeble resources to it. Three problems presented themselves to him. He wanted types less fragile than wooden types and less costly than engraving. He wanted a press by the aid of which he could obtain a clear impression on parchment or paper. He desired also that the leaves of his books should not be anopistograph, or printed only on one side. There were many unknown things to vex his soul, of which he himself alone could have a presentiment. Until then, and even long after, the xylographs were printed *au frotton* or with a brush, rubbing the paper upon the forme coated with ink, thicker than ordinary ink. He dreamed of something better.

In the course of his work John Gutenberg returned to Mayence. The idea of publishing a Bible, the Book of books, had taken possession of his heart. The *Spiegelmacher* of Strasbourg was on the road to loss. The cutting of his types had ruined him, and on his arrival in his native town, his stock in trade, transported by him, was of no great weight: some boxes of type, an inconvenient forme, and perhaps an ordinary press, a wine-maker's press, with a wooden screw. The idea of using this unwieldy instrument for the impression of his formes had already occurred to him; but would not the *frotton* serve still better? The force of the blow from the bar would break the miserable type, the raised parts of which could not resist the repeated strokes. In this unhappy situation, Gutenberg made the acquaintance of a financier of

Mayence, named Fust, who was in search of a business, and who put a sum of eleven hundred florins at his disposal to continue his experiments. Unfortunately this money disappeared, it melted away, and the results obtained were absolutely ludicrous.

It is certain that John Fust did not enter on the engagement without protecting himself. From the first he bound his debtor in a contract for six per cent. interest, besides a share in the profits. In addition he stipulated repayment in case of failure. Gutenberg, improvident, as is the way of inventors, had signed away all that he possessed to procure funds. It is presumed, besides, that during the continuance of his investigations, he composed some current books with the resources at his disposal, that served a little to lighten his debts. But the printing house of the Zum Jungen at Mayence was far from shining in the world, because the association of Fust concerned itself only with the publication of a Bible, and not at all with the *Speculums* and *Donatuses* that were so much in vogue at this time. Besides, the money-lender made a point of pressing his debtor, and did not allow him any leisure to labour outside the projected work. About this time a third actor enters on the scene. Peter Schoeffer, of Gernsheim, a writer, introduced into the workshop of Gutenberg to design letters, benefited by the abortive experiments, and taking up the invention at its deadlock, conducted it to success. John of Tritenheim, called Trithemius, the learned abbot of Spanheim, is the person who relates these facts; but as he got his information from Schoeffer himself, too much credence must not be given to his statements. Besides, Schoeffer was not at all an ordinary artisan. If we credit a Strasbourg manuscript written by his hand in 1449, he was a student of the "most glorious university of Paris." In the workshop of Gutenberg, his industrious and inventive intellect found a fecund mine, and this caligraphist dreamt of other things than shaping letters for the use of wood engravers. Gutenberg, arrested in his career by the wants of life, the worries of business, and perhaps also the fatigues of his labours, may have let the new-comer know something of his experiences. One cannot know, but it is certain that, shortly after, John Fust was so fascinated by Schoeffer, so attracted by his youth and his application, that he resolved to put new capital into the business. He did more: to permanently attach him, he gave him his grand-daughter in marriage, not his daughter, as was thought until M. Auguste Bernard rectified this mistake.

We have now come to 1453, the year preceding the first dated monument of printing in movable types: *the letters of indulgence*. It may be acknowledged that the sudden affection of Fust for his workman depended on some interested motive, and not at all on attraction of the heart. Had this former student of the university of Paris found the means of rapidly founding metallic types, the search for which had cost Gutenberg many sleepless nights? Had he completed it by applying to it the matrix and punch which had then and for centuries served the makers of seals and the money-coiners? Perhaps, as was most probable, the two associates had agreed, and putting their experiences together, had conquered hitherto insurmountable difficulties.

The year 1454 witnessed the diffusion throughout Christendom of letters of indulgence, accorded by Pope Nicholas V., who wished to aid in funds the King of Cyprus against the Turks. These circular letters, scattered by thousands to every corner of the world, employed numerous copyists. Arrived at Mayence, the distributers found a workshop ready prepared to furnish copies in the shortest possible time. They set to work and brought together all the type they possessed, cast or engraved, to set up these famous letters. Among the impressions was that of which we give a reproduction, which belongs to the edition called that of thirty-one lines. The original was delivered for a consideration to Josse Ott von Mospach on the 31st of December, 1454.

It is not without interest, for the history of the Book and of printing, to note here that these letters of indulgence, the clandestine traffic in which was largely accelerated by rapidity of production and the small cost of each copy, formed one of the causes of the religious reform of Martin Luther. They afforded a means of raising money, and were so generally resorted to that in the register of the Hotel de Ville of Paris preserved in the Archives Nationales (H 1778) it may be seen that the sheriffs requested the Pope to allow them to employ them in the reconstruction of the bridge at the Hotel de Ville.

The ice once broken, Fust and Schoeffer found it hard to nourish a useless mouth. For them Gutenberg was more of a hindrance than a profit, and they sought brutally to rid themselves of him. Fust had a most easy pretext, which was to demand purely and simply from his associate the sums advanced by him, and which had produced so little. Gutenberg had probably commenced his Bible, but, in face of the claims of Fust, he had to abandon it altogether, types, formes, and press.

Fig. 4.—Letters of indulgence, from the so-called edition of thirty-one lines, printed at Mayence in the course of 1454.

In November, 1455, he had retired to a little house outside the city, where he tried his best, by the aid of foreign help, to establish a workshop, and to preserve the most perfect secrecy. Relieved of his company, Fust and Schoeffer were able to take up the impression of the Bible and to complete it without him. If matters did so happen, and Schoeffer had not the excuse that he had previously discovered the casting of type, there is but one word to designate his conduct: robbery, and moral robbery, the worst of all. But what can be said to-day of these people?

One thing is certain: that the Bible of Schoeffer, commenced by Gutenberg or not, put on sale by Fust and Schoeffer alone about the end of 1455 or beginning of 1456, proves to be the first completed book. Retired to his new quarters, Gutenberg was taking courage, so as not to appear too much behindhand, but the reconstitution of his workshop cost him enormous time. And, besides, he missed the letter-maker Schoeffer, his own Gothic letters, engraved on steel with a punch, not having the same elegance. When his work appeared, it could not sustain comparison. The Bible of Schoeffer was more compact, the impression was more perfect, the ink better, the type less irregular. The original inventor, in his business with Fust, made an unhappy competition for himself. We give here a fragment of this celebrated book, a kind of mute witness of the science and mortifications of the first printer. It is now called the Mazarine Bible, from the fact that the copy in the Mazarin Library was the first to give evidence concerning it. The book was put on sale at the end of 1455 or beginning of 1456, for a manuscript note of a vicar of St. Stephen at Mayence records that he finished the binding and illuminating of the first volume on St. Bartholomew's Day, 1456, and the second on the 15th of August. St. Bartholomew's Day is the 13th of June, and not the 24th of August, as the catalogue of the Bibliothèque Nationale has it.

doctrina tenera adhuc et lactens· virum
iusti erudit infantia. Primus apud eos
liber· vocatur bresith: quem nos genesim
dicimus. Secundus ellesmoth: qui exodus
appellatur. Tercius vagetra: id est leviticus.
Quartus vagedaber: quem numeri voca-
mus. Quintus elleaddabarim: quod deuterono-
mium prenotatur. Hii sunt quinque libri moysi:
quos proprie thorath id est legem appellant.
Secundum prophetarum ordinem faciunt: et incipi-
unt ab ihesu filio nave: qui apud illos
iosue bennum dicitur. Deinde subtexunt
sopthim id est iudicum librum: et in eundem
compingunt ruth· quia in diebus iudicum:
facta eius narratur historia. Tercius sequi-
tur samuel: quem nos regnorum primum et
secundum dicimus. Quartus malachim id est

Fig. 5.—Fragment of the Mazarine Bible, printed in two columns. Beginning of the text in the second column; original size.

All these remarks show that the printers did not proclaim themselves, and were making pseudo-manuscripts. They did not make known their names or address. The rubricators sided with them, for many of the copies are illuminated with as much care and beauty as if they were the finest manuscripts.

There is no record extant of the number of copies printed, but it was done on both vellum and paper. Copies are by no means uncommon, most of the great libraries having one, and many are in private collections. One is shown among the typographical monuments in the King's Library of the British Museum, and there is a finely illuminated copy in the show-room of the Bibliothèque Nationale. From its very great importance as the first book that is known to have been printed, its value has a constant increase. Of the copies recently sold, one at the Perkins sale in 1873 on vellum sold for £3,400, another on paper at the same sale fetched £2,900, while one on paper in the Syston Park Library sold in December, 1884, for £3,900. It has been asserted that the copies on paper were the first issued by Gutenberg and his partners, and those on vellum subsequently printed by Fust and Schoeffer, after they had obtained possession of the inventor's stock.

But so many copies absolutely similar in aspect, and of so regular a style, put in the market from day to day by Fust and Schoeffer, gave rise to protests from the caligraphists. Criticism always attends upon success, but having obtained the result, the two associates did not hesitate to proclaim themselves the printers of the Bible. On the publication of the Psalter, which followed the Bible at a year's interval, they gave their names and added a date, 1457, the first instance of a date being recorded in a book. This second work was of so skilful a typography, that it might have been shown as the work of an expert penman; the faults remarked in the letters of indulgence are no longer seen; type had attained perfection; in two years printing had reached its culminating point.

In spite of his disappointments, Gutenberg did not rest idle. If he had seen his two enemies rob him of his claim of priority in the invention, he had to show that, reduced to his own exertions and to the restricted means furnished him by charitable people, he also could print well. Two years after the Bible a dated book, composed in Gothic letters, appeared at Mayence; this was the *Catholicon* of John Balbus, of Genoa. It had not yet occurred to these first printers to exercise their art otherwise than on religious works. It is admitted by general opinion that the *Catholicon* issued from the press of Gutenberg; on the other hand, M. Bernard believes that it ought to be attributed to a printer of Eltvil, who published in 1467 a vocabulary called the *Vocabularium ex quo* with the same types. The former theory may be sustained by the words of the colophon of the book, which is a sort of hymn to God and a recognition of the city of Mayence without any mention of the name of the printer. Now in the situation in which Gutenberg found himself, in the face of his rivals, had he not some claim to regard the great discovery as his own? But if M. Bernard is mistaken, and if our supposition has no foundation, what a beautiful act of humility, what a noble idea of his character, Gutenberg gives us in writing, "With the aid of the Most High, Who releases the tongues of infants and often reveals to babes that which is sealed to learned men, this admirable book the *Catholicon* was finished in the year of the incarnation of our Saviour MCCCCLX. in the mother-country of Mayence, famous city of Germany, which God, in His clemency, has deigned to render the most illustrious and the first of cities; and this book was perfected without the usual help of pen or style, but by the admirable linking of formes and types"!

Altissimi presidio cuius nutu infantium lingue fi
unt diserte.Qui eq nimiosepe puulis reuelat quod
sapientibus celat.Hic liber egregius.catholicon.
dnice incarnacionis annis M cccc lx Alma in ur
be maguntina nacionis inclite germanice.Quam
dei clemencia tam alto ingenij lumine.dono qz gra
tuito.ceteris terrarum nacionibus preferre.illustrare
qz dignatus est Non calami.stili.aut penne suffra
gio.s; mira patronarum formarum qz concordia pporcione et modulo.impressus atqz confectus est.
Hinc tibi sancte pater nato cum flamine sacro.Laus
et honor dno trino tribuatur et uno Ecclesie lau
de libro hoc catholice plaude Qui laudare piam
semper non linque mariam DEO.GRACIAS

Fig. 6.—Colophon of the *Catholicon*, supposed to have been printed by Gutenberg in 1460.

The history of these men, it is easy to understand, has to be regarded with caution, people of so little consequence then that the authentic documents relating to them have for ever disappeared. If we except that of the Pfennigthurm of Strasbourg, of which we have before spoken, and the deed of claim for money from Fust to Gutenberg dated 1455, we are forced to quote from authors living long afterwards, who submitted, without knowing better, to the miserable errors of oral tradition. It is nearly always the same with men who have occupied a large place in the history of art; posterity only knows of their genius at the time when no one knows anything of them. For Gutenberg the situation was still more terrible; a rival, Peter Schoeffer, survived him, and he did not for his own reputation care to preserve his rival's memory; and if, as is believed, Gutenberg left pupils and heirs, Henry Bechtermuncze, Ulrich Zell, and Weigand Spyes, his misfortune is crowned by Bechtermuncze being now reputed to be the printer of the *Catholicon*, of which we have just given the history. Even Albert Pfister, one of his workmen, dismissed at the end of his work, having obtained from his master some rejected types, was presumed later to have invented printing. We find this artisan established at Bamberg about 1460, composing Bibles in movable types, the first known being that published in 1461. But Albert Pfister showed that he was not at all an inventor by the mediocrity of his work, and more by the old types that he used. If he had known the secret of engraving the punches, he would have cast new letters and have given a better aspect to his work.

Presens hoc opusculum finitum ac completum et ad
eusebiam dei industrie in ciuitate Maguntij
per Johannem fust ciuem et Petrum schoiffher de
gernßheym clericum diocesis eiusdem est consu
matum. Anno incarnacionis dnice M.cccc.lxij.
In vigilia assumpcionis gloriose virginis marie.

Fig. 7.—Colophon of the Bible printed in 1462 by Fust and Schoeffer, which is the first dated Bible. There are two different editions with this signature. The above is from the second edition.

In these statements all is supposition and contradiction. That which is certain—and the dates are there to prove it—is the enormous progress in the productions of Peter Schoeffer. In 1459 he published his third book, Durand's *Rationale Divinorum Officiorum*, in folio. As in the Psalter, Schoeffer employed initial letters printed in red, which the rival workshop could not do in the *Catholicon*, the rubrics of which are painted by hand, as in manuscripts. In time he put forth a second edition of the Psalter, always with Fust's name joined to his own. A great number of types were broken at the beginning, but he dreamed of doing yet better. In 1460 he gave the *Constitutiones* of Pope Clement V., with a gloss and commentaries by John André; here was the first example of a process much employed in manuscripts, but of which the typographical composition was very difficult. Again, in 1462 a new Latin Bible issued from their workshops in two folio volumes. It is the first dated edition. The first volume has two hundred and forty-two folios in double columns, the second two hundred and thirty-nine. It commences with an epistle of St. Jerome, and on the last leaf of the second volume is the colophon on the preceding page.

This book, one of the first worthy of the name, and which is called by preference the Mayence Bible, appeared in one of the most troubled epochs that the episcopal city had had to go through. Subject to its archbishops, who were at the head of all the lay lords and fighting men, the city found itself in 1462 the prey of two prelates of equal title who refused to give way to one another: Thierry of Isembourg and Adolph of Nassau-Wiesbaden. Adolph surprised Mayence on the 27th October, 1462, pursuing his adversary, who scaled the walls with a rope to escape quicker, and the city was sacked and pillaged from its foundations. In the middle of this turmoil, what became of the obscure persons who were then the printers of the Bible? Doubtless their insignificance saved them from disaster, but as it was long before peace was re-established, and the entire edition of their last volume could not be kept back, we incline to believe that they were for a time going about the country as itinerant booksellers. Paris was to them a well-indicated point of travel—Paris, toward which all German commerce tended. The university where Peter Schoeffer was instructed in letters, and that truly passed for the first in Europe, appeared to them a market of the first order. If we may believe Walchius (*Decas fabularum generis humani*: Strasbourg, 1609, 4to, p. 181), John Fust himself went to that city, where he put books on sale from sixty crowns a copy, then fifty, then forty, according to the prevailing system in matters of discount. Fust was above all things a merchant; he led it to be believed that he had the marvellous establishment of a copyist beyond the Rhine, and he had disposed of many copies, when the corporate scribes of the university, becoming aware of the imposition, cried out furiously and declared it a diabolical invention. We may now take this tale of Walchius as a fable, as the registers of Parliament, on being consulted, rest silent on the proceedings instituted against the "magician" of Mayence. Only we must not lose sight of the fact that the booksellers had their masters, their syndicate, if we may use the modern word, charged to prohibit fraudulent publications. They were too much interested in the suppression of printed books to judge the matter coldly. The Parliament had nothing to see to in this.

The revolution of Mayence had otherwise great results, which were not affected by these minor reverses. The printing workshops, or at least the successors of Gutenberg, began to be dispersed, and Fust and Schoeffer having established a school of printers in the city, their trade was no longer secret. Deprived of their liberties by the new Archbishop, many of them expatriated themselves. We shall take occasion later to name some of these exiles, through whom the art of printing spread itself almost simultaneously throughout the world: to Cologne and Strasbourg, to Italy and Spain, without reckoning Holland, France, Switzerland, and the country around Mayence. We have before named the episcopal city of Bamberg; it had the singular fortune to be the second city to possess a printing office, but it disappeared as quickly as it was established, with Albert Pfister, without leaving the least trace; we do not find printing there again before 1480, more than twenty years later.

Gutenberg was dead before 1468. He was interred in the Church of the Récollets of Mayence, by the pious care of a friend, who attributed the invention of printing to him on his tomb.

We may begin to comprehend the influence of this man upon the discovery of which all the world was then talking, but the troubles of the archiepiscopal city hampered the respective merit of the inventors. Peter Schoeffer and John Fust were not much affected by the political crisis. After two years' suspension, they reappeared with a Cicero, *De Officiis*, 1465, quarto, always at work and always surpassing themselves. This time they freely gave up religious publications, and, still more extraordinary, they employed Greek types.

Such is, detached from the incredible contradictions of writers on art, and sketched solely on its main lines, the origin of printing as it is established at this day. First came the image engraved in relief, which we have not gone to China to find, with some of our predecessors. Upon this image were often cut, by the same economical process, legends of explanation that presented the idea of imitation of manuscript; and the xylographs appeared with or without illustrations. Then from the correction of errors in these books followed the discovery of movable characters. This wooden type, possible when it was used with a *frotton* for printing, would quickly break under the press, the idea of which was gained from the common press of the wine-makers. Then a kind of metallic type had to be found which would run in a mould struck by a punch. This punch was not invented for the purpose; it served previously for the makers of coins and seals. The fabrication of type from the matrix was a simple adoption. The lead thrown into the matrix gave the desired type. Thus were made the first books, of which we have briefly related the composition.

As to the proportion of glory due to each one of the first printers, it is necessary equally, to guard against error on one side or the other. We have sought to separate from the heap of publications probable opinions or those based on certain documents. That the origin of the *Donatus*, the block books, was Dutch would be puerile to deny, because, on one side, the engravings on blocks are surely of the school of Van Eyck, and, on the other hand, Ulrich Zell, who inspired the "Cologne Chronicle" of 1499, assigned positively to Holland the cradle of the *Donatus*. At any rate, it was a pupil of Gutenberg, a question we have discussed. After that we will trouble ourselves but little about Laurent Coster. The name makes no difference in a matter of this kind.

As to Gutenberg, we have not been able to go as far as M. E. Dutuit, who in his *Manuel a'Estampes* (vol. i., p. 236, etc.) doubts Gutenberg's right to the title of inventor. It is stated that in a letter of William Fichet, prior of the Sorbonne, of whom we shall have more to say presently, to Robert Gaguin, which M. A. Claudin found at the beginning of a work entitled *Gasparim Pergamensis orthographiæ liber*, published in 1470, nearly twenty years after the first work at Mayence, Gutenberg is proclaimed the inventor of printing. Without any other, this testimony of a *savant* who was the first to bring the German printers to Paris appears to us well nigh irrefutable.

As to John Fust and his grandson by marriage, Peter Schoeffer, they are so well defended by their works, that there is no more to say here; doubtless grave presumptions arise as to the delicacy of their conduct with Gutenberg, but we are not so bold as to censure them beyond measure. We know nothing precise either of the time or of the men.

Let us now imagine humble workmen, the most simple of *gens de mestiers*, to employ the French expression then in use, shut up in a kind of dark workshop, like a country forge, formed in little groups of two or three persons, one designing and the other cutting the wood, having near them a table, on which is held the engraved block after its reliefs have been rubbed with sombre ink, who afterwards, by means of the *frotton*, apply the damped paper to the raised parts of the block; we shall have without much stretch of thought all the economy of the xylographic impression. If we add to this primitive workshop the matrix in which the types are cast, the box in which they are distributed, the forme on which they are arranged to compose the pages, and a small hand-press, with blacker ink and paper damped to permit the greasy ink to take better, we have a picture of the work-room of Gutenberg, Fust, and Schoeffer, and of the first printers with movable types.

Thus typography was born of painting, passing in its infancy through wood-cutting, revolutionising ideas and somewhat the world. But the mighty power of the new art was not confined to itself; it extended the circle of engraving, which till then had suffered from the enormous difficulties of reproduction. As if the time were ripe for all these things, nearly at the moment when the first printers were distinguishing themselves by serious works, a Florentine goldsmith accidentally discovered the cutting of cast metal.[1] What would have become of this new process if the presses of Gutenberg had not brought their powerful assistance to the printing of engravings? It will be found then that printing rendered a hundredfold to engraving for that which it received from it and bore it along with its own rapid advance.

Then reappeared, following the new processes, the figures somewhat abandoned by the Mayence workmen during the period of transformation. Our object is to speak at length of the Book ornamented and illustrated according to the means of relief-cutting or casting; to demonstrate the influence of painting, of sculpture, of art, on the production of the Book; and thus to help the reader at the same time to understand the almost sudden and irresistible development of typography, and to mention its foremost representatives.

[1] The opinion that Finiguerra was the unconscious inventor of casting engravings is now abandoned.

CHAPTER II.

1462 TO 1500.

The Book and the printers of the second generation—The German workmen dispersed through Europe—Caxton and the introduction of printing into England—Nicholas Jenson and his supposed mission to Mayence—The first printing in Paris; William Fichet and John Heinlein—The first French printers; their installation at the Sorbonne and their publications—The movement in France—The illustration of the Book commenced in Italy—The Book in Italy; engraving in relief and metal plates—The Book in Germany: Cologne, Nuremberg, Basle—The Book in the Low Countries—French schools of ornament of the Book; Books of Hours; booksellers at the end of the fifteenth century—Literary taste in titles in France at the end of the fifteenth century—Printers and booksellers' marks—The appearance of the portrait in the Book—Progress in England—Caxton and his followers.

ONSIDERING the influence of printing on the book trade of the fifteenth century, as referred to in the preceding pages, the dealers in manuscripts were not disposed to give way at the first blow. An entire class of workmen would find themselves from day to day without employment if the new art succeeded; these were the copyists, miserable scribes, who for meagre remuneration frequented the shops of the merchants, where they transcribed manuscripts by the year. Before printing the publication of books was so effected, and the booksellers were rather intermediaries between the copyist and the buyer, than direct dealers having shops and fittings complete. It is evident that they would not provide themselves with these costly books long in advance without being sure of disposing of them.

Small as was the remuneration of the writers, it was much to them; and they were naturally the first to protest against the new invention. At the same time, their opposition and that of the booksellers was soon overcome, swamped, and choked by the growing crowd of printers. Then, as always happens in similar cases, in place of fighting against the current, most of the former workers in manuscript followed it. The writers designed letters for engraving in wood, the booksellers sold the printed works, and some of the illuminators engraved in relief or cast their *histoyres*. For a long time these last continued to decorate books with the ornamental drawings with which they had adorned the manuscripts, and so contributed to form the fine school of illustrators who carried their art to so high a point from the end of the fifteenth century.

As previously related, the revolution of Mayence caused the flight of a crowd of artisans who found their liberty suddenly compromised by the conqueror. The want of money at this time always brought a diminution of patronage, and working printers have been at all times tenacious of their privileges. It so happened that their guild, in place of remaining established at Mayence many years longer, was, as it were, turned out, scattered to the four cardinal points by the dispersion of its members, and scattered many years before the natural time. In point of fact, in the common order of things, a workman here and there quits the principal workshop to try the world. He makes his way timidly, unconscious apostle of a marvellous art. If he succeeds, he gathers some pupils round him; if he fails, no trace of him remains; in any case invention propagates itself more gradually. With printing it was a thunderclap. Hardly had it made its appearance when the exodus commenced. The greater part of the Mayence men went to Italy: to Subiaco and to Rome, Arnold Pannartz, Conrad Sweynheim, Ulrich Hahn; to Venice, John of Spire, Vendelin of Spire, Christopher Valdarfer, Bernard Pictor (of Augsburg), Erhardt Ratdolt, Peter Loslein; to Ferrara, Andrew Belfort; to Foligno, John Neumeister; Henry Alding tried Sicily; Andrew Vyel, of Worms, printed at Palermo. Lambert Palmart was at Valencia, in Spain, in 1477; Nicholas Spindeler at Barcelona; Peter Hagenbach at Toledo; not far from Mayence—that is, at Cologne—Ulrich Zell, a pupil of Gutenberg, who dated his first work 1466. It was Arnold Ther Hoernen who numbered a book with Arabic figures; it was Koelhof who first used signatures to indicate to the binder the order of the sheets; it was at Eltvil that Henry Bechtermuncze, as we have already said, printed his *Vocabularium* in German, with the types of the *Catholicon*; at Basle, Berthold Rüppel, of Hanau, was the first established in that city which after Mayence did the most for printing; at Nuremberg, Koburger, who took nearly the first rank among his contemporaries, set as many as twenty-four presses to work, and was named by Badius the prince of printers. And how matters went on! For instance, the very year that followed the death of Gutenberg, monks, the Brothers of the Common Life of Marienthal, in the Rheingau, themselves published a copy of the indulgences accorded by Adolph of Nassau, Archbishop of Mayence. Before 1480, presses were everywhere in Germany: at Prague, Augsburg, Ulm, Lubeck, Essling, etc.

Explicit presens vocabulorum
materia · a per docto eloquentissimo
qz viro · dño Gherardo de schueren.
Cācellario Illustrissimi ducis Cli
uensis ex diuersorum terministarum
voluminibus contexta · propriisqz
eiusdem manibus labore ingenti cō
scripta ac correcta Colonie per me
Arnoldū ther hornē diligentissime
impressa · finita sub annis domini ·
M · cccc · lxxvij · die vltimo mensis
maij · De quo cristo marie filio sit
laus et gloria per seculorum secula
Amen · :·

Fig. 8.—Imprint of Arnold Ther Hoernen, printer, of Mayence.

It is to be remarked that the Mayence men did not turn towards Holland. Is it that they found there the descendants of Laurent Coster firmly established in their workshops? Must the coexistence, the simultaneous advance, of the invention in Germany and in the Low Countries be admitted? It is a secret for us and for many others, but we know for certain that Flemish printers were established at Utrecht in 1473, at Delft, Bruges, Gouda, Zwoll, Antwerp, and Brussels. At Louvain there was besides John of Westphalia, who published in 1474 a work of Peter Crescens, and several other works.

Colard Mansion was printing at Bruges about 1473; and was employed by William Caxton, who had been for some years trading as a merchant in the Low Countries, to print the "Recuyell of the Histories of Troy," by Raoul Le Fevre, which Caxton had translated into English at the command of Queen Margaret. This was issued in 1474, and was the first book printed in the English language. In 1475 or 1476 Caxton returned to England with a fount of types, which he had employed Mansion to cut and cast for him, and established himself as a printer in the precincts of Westminster Abbey. In 1477 he produced the first book printed in England, "The Dictes and Sayings of the Philosophers," followed by a large number of important works, many of them written or translated by Caxton himself. Thus was typography firmly established in England; and Caxton's immediate successors, Wynken de Worde, Richard Pynson, William Machlinia, have had a glorious roll of followers, which has never been broken to this day. From Westminster the art spread in England to Oxford, where Theodoricus Rood, from Cologne, printed an *Exposicio Sancti Jeronimi* in 1478; and to St. Albans in 1480 by a printer who has never been identified, and who produced the famous "Chronicle" and "Boke of St. Albans."

The invasion, we see, had been most rapid. In less than fifteen years, every important city had followed the movement, and was ready to establish printing offices. If we may credit a certain controverted document, Charles VII. had on the 3rd of October, 1458, sent to Mayence one of the best medal engravers of the Mint of Tours to study the process of which marvels were spoken: "The 3rd of October, 1458, the King having learned that Messire Guthenberg, living at Mayence, in the country of Germany, a dexterous man in carving and making letters with a punch, had brought to light the invention of printing by punches and types, desirous of inquiring into such a treasure, the King has commanded the generals of his mints to nominate persons well instructed in the said cutting and to send them secretly to the said place to inform themselves of the said mode and invention, to understand and learn the art of them, in order to satisfy the said Lord King; and it was undertaken by Nicholas Jenson, who took the said journey to bring intelligence of the said art and of the execution of it in the said kingdom, which first has made known the said art of impression to the said kingdom of France" (Bibliothèque de l'Arsenal, Hf 467, pp. 410, 411).

Nicholas Jenson on his return met with a cool reception from Louis XI., who did not continue the works of his father. It may be supposed that this coolness was the cause of his expatriating himself and retiring to a place where his industry could be better exercised. Ten years after the above mission we find him established at Venice, his art of engraver of letters joined to that of printer. His Eusebius, translated by Trapezuntius, and his Justinian, were composed in 1470 with such marvellous and clear types that from that day the best typographers have imitated his founts. In spite of its success, he did not confine himself to these letters, but he made use also of Gothic, in which he printed by preference pious books.

barbarum ac ferum legibus ad cultioré uitæ usum
traductũ in formã prouĩnciæ redegit.

.FINIS.

Historias ueteres peregrinaq; gesta reuoluo
Iustinus. lege me: sum trogus ipse breuis.
Me gallus ueneta Ienson Nicolaus in urbe
Formauit: Mauro principe Christophoro.

IVSTINI HISTORICI CLARISSIMI IN
TROGI POMPEII HISTORIAS LIBER
XLIIII. FELICITER EXPLICIT.

.M.CCCC.LXX.

Fig. 9.—Imprint of Nicholas Jenson to a Justinian, printed in 1470 at Venice. This type has prevailed up to now.

In spite of the attempts of Jenson in the name of the King of France—that is, if these attempts ever took place in the manner indicated above—the invention was not known to have commended itself to the powerful university of Paris. In general, and especially for the introduction of innovations in that learned body, it was necessary to fight, to strike without much chance of success, save in case of having acquaintance in the place. We have seen John Fust, obliged suddenly to retake the road to Germany, in a fair way to find himself taxed with sorcery, not an inconsiderable matter. For others the sale of unauthorised books had had most unhappy consequences unless the Parliament intervened. So ten years had passed since the journey of Jenson, and ten or twelve since the first manifestations of typography at Mayence, without the diabolical discovery finding admittance to the Sorbonne. A still more extraordinary thing, a Cologne printer issued about 1472 a small folio in Gothic type, thirty-one long lines to a page, which was a work written in French. The *Histoires de Troyes* of Raoul Le Fevre, chaplain of the dukes of Burgundy, first found a publisher in Germany, and soon after another in England, before a single press was definitely installed at Paris.

As we have said of Peter Schoeffer, numerous German students were in the university, where they pursued their studies, and frequently remained later as masters. It has been found that in 1458 a former student of Leipzig named John Heinlein, a native of Stein, in the diocese of Spire, entered as regent of the college of Burgundy, from whence he passed to the Sorbonne in 1462, the year of the troubles in Mayence. After the manner of latinising names so common at that time, he called himself Lapidanus, from the name of his native place, which means Stone in German. Heinlein met in Paris a Savoyard, William Fichet, born in 1433 at Petit Bornand, who became an associate of the Sorbonne about 1461, and finally rector in 1468. These two men were great friends, and their particular instincts attracted them to men of elevated studies. They divined at once the enormous help printing would bring to their work. Besides, it grieved them to see through the whole of France, especially in Touraine, German colporteurs carrying on their trade under cover of other commerce, a practice from which the most grave inconveniences might result. It occurred to them that to prevent fraud they would themselves create a printing establishment; but if they deliberated on it, it must have been in secret, for the registers of the Sorbonne are silent on their enterprise. If Fichet conceived the idea, it may be believed that, from his German origin, Heinlein put it into execution. M. Philippe thinks that he was formerly at Basle. In all probability it was from that city he tried to obtain his workmen. In 1468 six years had elapsed since the craftsmen were dispersed and fled from Mayence. At all events, it was from Basle that Ulrich Gering, Michael Freyburger, and Martin Krantz, printers recommended to the two

Sorbonnists, departed, and in due course arrived in Paris. Of these three men, who were the first to establish a printing office on the French side of the Rhine, Ulrich Gering was a student as well as a printer, so was Freyburger, originally of Colmar. Krantz was a letter-founder, and the only real workman of the three companions.

We have often regretted with regard to these men, as also to Gutenberg, Fust, and Schoeffer, that no really authentic portrait has transmitted their features to us. Every one will recall the fur cap and loose pantaloons of the mediocre statue at Mayence, but there is really no portrait of Gutenberg. As to Gering, M. Philippe, in his *Histoire de l'Origine de l'Imprimerie à Paris*, publishes a grotesque figure muffled in the ruff of the sixteenth century, after a picture preserved at Lucerne, but for which much cannot be said. Lacaille, in his *Histoire de l'Imprimerie*, gives a full-length portrait of Gering, said to be taken from a painting in the College Montagu.

The workshop of the three Germans was set up within the walls of the Sorbonne—*in ædibus Sorbonnicis*—in 1469. There they set to work at once, their printing establishment consisting simply of a room, none too light, a table, a press, and formes. Krantz doubtless struck the types chosen by the Sorbonnists, for there were then in use two sorts of letters: German Gothic and Roman. They kept to the Roman, as being more round and clear; and as soon as they obtained matrices and cast their type, they entered on their task with ardour.

The tendencies of Fichet and Heinlein were not towards transcendent theology, but rather towards the literature of the ancients and contemporary rhetorical works. Besides, it may be said, considering that men are far from perfect, Fichet counted on making the authorised presses serve his own purpose. We find him publishing a treatise on rhetoric in quarto in 1471; meantime he supervised the work confided to his artists. They commenced with a large volume of "Letters" of Gasparin of Bergamo, which was set up in quarto with the Roman type, the form of which had been accepted. At the end of the work, the impression of which cost much time—possibly a year—the three printers placed a quatrain in Latin distichs, which is at once a statement of identity and a promise for the future.

Gaſparini pergamenſis clariſſimi orato/
riſ, epiſtolarum liber foeliciter incipit;

Audeo plurimum ac lætor in
ea te ſententia eſſe: ut nihil a
me fieri ſine cauſa puteſ. Ego
enī etſi multorum uerebar ſuſpi/
tioneſ, q a me ſemproniū antiquū fami/
liarē meū reiiciebā: tamē cū ad incredibi/
lē animi tui ſapiētiā iudiciū meū refere/
bā: nihil erat q̄re id a te improbari pu/
tarem. Nam cum & meoſ noſſeſ moreſ: &
illius naturā ñ ignorareſ: ñ dubitabā qd
de hoc facto meo iudicaturus eſſes. Non
igitur haſ ad te ſcribo lrāſ, quo nouam tibi
de rebuſ a me geſtiſ opinionem faciā: ſed
ut ſi quando aliter homīeſ noſtroſ de me
ſētire intelliges: tu q probe cauſam meā
noſti, defenſionē meā ſuſcipiaſ. Hæc ſi fe/
ceris: nihil eſt quo ulterius officium tu/
um requiram. Vale;

Fig. 10.—"Letters" of Gasparin of Bergamo. First page of the first book printed at Paris, in 1470.

Foelix Epiſtolarum Gaſparini finis.

Ut ſol lumen, ſic doctrinam fundiſ in orbem
Muſarum nutrix, regia pariſiuſ;
Hinc prope diuinam, tu quā germania nouit
Artem ſcribendi: ſuſcipe promerita;
Primos ecce libroſ: quos hæc induſtria finxit
Francorum in terriſ, ædibuſ atque tuiſ;
Michael, Udalricuſ, Martinuſque magiſtri
Hoſ impreſſerunt, ac facient alioſ;

Fig. 11.—Colophon in distichs in the "Letters" of Gasparin of Bergamo, first book printed at Paris, at the office of the Sorbonne.

If we try to apportion to each of the three printers his share in the making of the book, it may be supposed that the intellectual part of the composition and the correction fell to Freyburger and Gering, while the heavier work of founding, placing in formes, and press work fell to Krantz. This essay, satisfactory as it appeared, was far from perfection. The first Parisian printers had multiplied abbreviations and irregular contractions, and enormous difficulties and inevitable faults ensued. Further, either they had more than one punch, or the leaden matrix was deformed, for the characters frequently differ. At the same time, we must commend them for having used the *æ* and *œ*, which were uniformly written *e* in the manuscripts, thus giving rise to errors without number. Their punctuation was the comma, semicolon, and full stop.

De quinque rhetoricis elementis artem extrinsecus comprehendentibus omnem.

ARtificiose dicendi ratio (quae latissime patet) quinque rebus ad summum conficitur: facultate, fine, officio, materia, et instrumento. Nam totidem rebus: qui reliquis artibus delectantur: limites sibi definiunt.

FACVLTAS (quae est certa, facilis, et prompta dicendi potestas) tribus rebus constat: arte, imitatione, et exercitatione.

ARS est praeceptio: quae dat certam uiam, rationemque dicendi.

IMITATIO est: qua impellimur cum diligenti ratione, quem, quid, et quantum imitemur: ut aliquorum similes in dicendo ualeamus esse.

EXERCITATIO est assiduus usus, consuetudoque dicendi.

FINIS est quae fit dictione persuasio.

OFFICIVM est: apposite dicere ad persuasionem. Quod opus partibus suis quinque consumimus: inuentione, dispositione, elocutione,

Fig. 12.—*Rhetorique* of Fichet, printed at Paris in 1471. The marginal ornaments are drawn by hand.

Fichet and Heinlein had become the modest librarians of the Sorbonne, and this new employment gave them greater facilities for surveillance. The printing office did not remain inactive. It issued successively the "Orthography" of Gasparin of Bergamo, the "Letters" of Phalaris, two books of Æneas Sylvius, the "Conspiracy of Catiline" of Sallust, the "Epitome of Titus Livius" of Florus, and finally the "Rhetorics" of William Fichet, which, if we may credit a letter addressed to Bessarion, was finished in 1471. Following came the "Letters" of Bessarion, the *Elegantia Latinæ Linguæ* of Valla, the first folio volume from the Sorbonne presses; and others, thirteen volumes in 1470-71 and seventeen in 1472.

At the end of 1472 the workshop was somewhat broken up, Fichet having left for Rome and Heinlein preaching in Germany. The three printers had shown by their works that they were in earnest; besides, they had from the first gratuitously distributed copies among the nobles, who, being accustomed to pay highly for manuscripts, did not fail to note the difference. The associates then resolved to quit the Sorbonne and create an establishment for themselves; their patrons being no longer there to sustain them in case of failure, and in giving up their presses and types it may be judged that they were not without anxiety on that point.

Their oldest dated book, the *Manipulus Curatorum* of Montrochet, was also the first that they printed in their new quarters, at the sign of the "Golden Sun" in the Rue St. Jacques. They remained united up to the year 1477, when Gering alone printed at the "Golden Sun," but he obtained associates, George Mainyal in 1480 and Berthold Rembold in 1494, who lived with him in the Rue de la Sorbonne, where he established himself on leaving the Rue St. Jacques. Ulrich Gering died on the 23rd of August, 1510, after a half-century of work.

The movement inaugurated by the Sorbonne was promptly followed. German workmen opened their shops nearly everywhere in France; then the French themselves scattered. At Lyons in 1472 a Frenchman was established, the same at Angers, Caen, Metz, Troyes, Besançon, and Salins. But in the central provinces we find Henry Mayer at Toulouse, John Neumeister at Albi; in the east Metlinger at Dijon; and Michael Wensler, of Basle, at Macon, among others, about 1493.

We have now arrived at an epoch of greater efforts. The Lyons printers used ornamental letters, from which were developed engravings in the Book. Since the block books illustration had been neglected, as the means were wanting to distribute the plates here and there in the forme; Schoeffer still employed initial letters in wood very like vignettes. John Fust was now dead, but Peter Schoeffer continued to print without intermission.

If we search for the precise epoch in which illustration appeared in the history of the Book, we shall perhaps have to go back to the time of Albert Pfister, printer of Bamberg, who issued in 1461 an edition of the "Fables of Ulrich Bohner" with a hundred and one figures on wood. This may be said to be the unconscious combination of xylography with typography, a kind of transformation of old elements to new things without other importance; art had no place in this adaptation.

Up to this time Germany had not, in its school of painters or miniaturists, men capable of giving a personal impulse to ornament. In the German editions of the block books the influence of Van Eyck had made itself felt very sensibly, and the Flemish had preserved their supremacy on this point; on the other hand, the German printers who went to seek their fortune in Italy fell into the middle of a circle admirably prepared to receive them and to communicate their ideas to them. It is believed that the first book printed in Italy with woodcuts in the text and with an ascertained date is the work of a German established at Rome, Ulrich Hahn, in 1467. An account in the *Annuaire du Bibliophile*, which, being without citation of authority, we quote for what it is worth, relates that Ulrich Hahn was established as a printer at Vienna about 1462, but was driven thence by the publication of a pamphlet against the burgomaster of the city, and was attracted to Rome by Torquemada, who confided to him the impression of his work the *Meditationes*. Hahn was an engraver, as were also most of his *confrères* at that time—that is, he cut in relief designs to be intercalated in the text—and Passavant relates that the designs of the *Meditationes* were from compositions of Fra Angelico, who died in 1455. Be that as it may, the book, the printing of which was finished on St. Sylvester's Day, 1467, is the first known with engravings, and only three copies of it exist: one at Vienna, one at Nuremberg, and one in Lord Spencer's library; it is composed in Gothic type in folio.

Fig. 13.—Wood engraving of Matteo Pasti for Valturius' *De Re Militari*: Verona, 1472.

Illustration found a true artist at Verona, Matteo Pasti, who furnished designs for a volume on military art by Valturius, printed in Roman characters in folio, at the expense of John of Verona, and dedicated to Sigismond Pandolfi. Pasti's eighty-two figures are simple outlines, and we here reproduce one of the principal—an archer shooting at a butt. Published in 1472, the volume of Valturius followed soon after the *Meditationes*, but the engravings enable us to see how the Italian process, consisting mostly of lines without shadows, differed from the Dutch and German. One thing to be remarked here is the purity of the design, in spite of the roughness of the engraving; we see in these figures Italian art at its height, despite the somewhat coarse translation of the wood-cutter.

At Venice the German inventors had reaped their harvest. At the end of the fifteenth century, fifty years after the invention of typography, the printing offices and booksellers' shops were counted by hundreds. It was in this city that for the first time a title with frontispiece carrying indication of the contents, the place, the date, and the name of the printer, was given to the Book. We give here this ornamental title, placed before a *Calendario* of John de Monteregio, printed by Pictor, Loslein, and Ratdolt in 1476, folio.

The German Erhardt Ratdolt was probably the promoter of these innovations. He soon afterwards published the first geometrical book with figures, the "Elements of Euclid," 1482, folio; in the same year he produced the *Poeticon Astronomicum* of Hyginus, previously printed at Ferrara, with illustrations on wood of excellent design, but laboriously and unskilfully engraved. Yet the art of the Book could not remain mediocre in this city, where the artists were creating marvels. John of Spire and afterwards Nicholas Jenson, the emigrant from France, of whom we have spoken above, had created, after Italian manuscripts, that Roman letter, the primitive type of which has come down to our time very little retouched. At the death of Jenson in 1481, his materials passed into the hands of Andrew d'Asola, called Andrea Torresani, who did not allow the good traditions of his master to die, and who produced among others a book bearing signatures, catchwords, and paging ("Letters of St. Jerome," 1488). Torresani was the father-in-law of Aldus Manutius, who was to be for ever illustrious in the art of printing at Venice, and raised his art to the highest perfection.

Questa opra da ogni parte e un libro doro
Non fu piu preciosa gemma mai
Dil kalendario : che tratta cose sfu
Con gran facilita : ma gran lauoro
Qui numero aureo : e tutti i segni fuoro
Descripti dal gran polo da ogni lat
Quando il sole : e luna eclipsi fa
Quante terre se tege a sto thesoro
In un instanti tu sai qual hora sia
Qual sara lanno : giorno : tempo : e mese :
Che tutti ponti son dastrologia
Ioanne de monte regio questo leve
Coglier tal frutto acio non graue sia
In breue tempo : e con pochi penese.
Chi teme cotal spese
Stampa ortu I nomi di impression
Son qui da basso di rossi colori

Venetijs. 1476.

Bernardus pictor de Augusta
Petrus loslein de Langencen
Erhardus ratdolt de Augusta

Fig. 14.—Title-page of the *Calendario*, first ornamental title known. Printed in 1476 at Venice.

But if decoration by means of relief blocks found a favourable reception in Italy and, above all, a group of artists capable of carrying it to success, there were at the same time other experiments conceived in a different way. The discovery of Maso Finiguerra gave to the art a new process of reproduction, and printing presses had now to render possible and practicable the working of engraved plates. In order to make that which follows comprehensible, we enter into a few technical details, the whole subject having been so admirably and fully treated by MM. Delaborde and Duplessis.

In the engraved wood block, as in the printing type, it is a projection in the wood or metal which, being inked and passed under a press, leaves on paper its lines in black. Naturally then the intercalation of an engraving of this kind in typographical composition is made without difficulty, and the impression of both is taken at once. On the other hand, a line engraving is obtained from incised lines on a plate of copper; that is, an instrument called a burin traces the lines, which are filled with greasy ink. These incised lines only are inked. The surface of the plate is cleaned off to avoid smudging. The sheet of paper destined for the impression has then to be made very pliable, so that at the striking of the press it runs, so to speak, to find the ink in the lines and hold it. It is therefore impossible to take a text from relief characters at the same time as an engraved plate.

Fig. 15.—Engraving on metal by Baccio Baldini for *El Monte Santo di Dio*, in 1477.

However, this kind of reproduction, which, contrary to that from wood, allowed of half-tints or toning down, attracted in good time the workers at the Book. It appeared to them possible to reconcile the two printings by the successive passage of the same sheet of paper through the press, to receive at first the impression from the type and afterwards to find the ink deposited in the incisions in the copper. The first manifestation of this new method of illustration was made at Florence, the home of line engraving, by Nicholas di Lorenzo in 1477, for the work of Antonio Bettini, of Siena, called *El Monte Santo di Dio*. Here the artists were never known. Common opinion has it that Baccio Baldini borrowed from Sandro Botticelli the subjects of his plates. Italian engraving always seeks its source in Pollajuolo, Botticelli, and Baldini. It is not the simple work of a niellist, but it had not yet reached perfection either in the work or in the impression; the illustrations of the *Monte Santo* are proof of this, as are also those of the *Dante*, by Baldini, in 1481, for the same Nicholas di Lorenzo. From this we reproduce the Misers.

Fig. 16.—Metal engraving by Baccio Baldini from the Dante of 1481.

At this epoch engravings from the burin were taken with a pale ink, the composition of which is very different from the fine black ink of Schoeffer as well as of the old Italian printers. And besides in most cases the proofs were obtained with the *frotton*, like the ancient block books, an eminently defective process. The press was not yet well adapted to the delicate work of line engraving, and the workmen, who did not apply the plates until after the text was printed, preferred not to risk the loss of their sheets by the use of inappropriate presses. These, with the insignificant attempts made by the Germans in 1479, [2] are the beginnings of the process of line engraving in the ornamentation of the Book. In fact, the process failed to take its due position for want of a more convenient mode of working. Relief engraving had got ahead; with it the sheets used for the impression did not require working more than once to register the figures with the text; in a word, the labour was not so great. A century had to pass before line engraving completely dethroned the vignette on wood, a century in which the latter attained its height, and showed what able artisans could make of a process apparently the least flexible.

[2] *Breviarium ecclesie Herbipolensis*: Et. Dold., 1479, folio, copper plate engravings.

Not to leave Italy, which had the honour of making the book with engraved illustrations known to the world, we pass by some years, during which Arnold Bucking gave at Rome a *Cosmographia* of Ptolemy, 1478, with incised plates, which is the first printed atlas that was produced, whilst as regards ordinary publications there appeared in all parts classical and Italian works, such as Cicero, Virgil, Tacitus, Pliny, Eusebius, among the ancients, and Dante, Petrarch, Boccaccio, etc., among moderns. Among the editions of Dante, we may cite that of Peter of Cremona, dated 18th November, 1491, with one engraving to each canto, of which the earlier are after Botticelli, and perhaps drawn by him directly on the wood. Passavant believes these figures to be cut in relief in the metal. On some of the plates there is a signature, a Gothic **b**, the signification of which leaves a free field for conjecture, and perhaps for error. Copies of this book with the complete series of twenty plates are extremely rare; one in the Hamilton Palace Library sold in May, 1884, for £380; the Royal Library of Berlin recently agreed to pay £1,200 for a proof set of the plates.

Fig. 17.—Plate from the *Hypnerotomachia Poliphili*, printed by Aldus Manutius, in 1499.

As we shall see later apropos of German vignettes of the same period, the characteristic of Italian engraving was sobriety, the complete absence of useless work and the great simplicity of the human figure. This special manner will be found in the famous edition of the *Hypnerotomachia Poliphili* of Francis Colonna, printed in 1499 by Aldus, copied sixty years later by a French printer, and lately reproduced in reduced size.

Fig. 18.—Plate from Bonino de Bonini's Dante, at Brescia, in 1487.

The Italian illustrators, whether they were working in wood, or, as some writers have it, in metal, adroitly brought their figures forward by contrasting some rudimentary work in the persons with the more accentuated and often stippled ground, which formed a dark background. This was also the ordinary process in their ornaments, among the most interesting of which are the borders of the plates to an edition of Dante by Bonino de Bonini, Brescia, 1487, of which a specimen is here reproduced.

If we return from Italy, which then took the lead, to Germany, a school of *Formschneiders* is found about the year 1470 at Augsburg, whose secluded workshops were of no benefit to the booksellers. These ill-advised artisans went still further. Apparently furious to see printing so widely spread as to render their bad woodcuts difficult to get rid of, they united in a body to interdict Gunther Zainer and Schüssler from putting engravings into their books. They must nevertheless have come to an ultimate arrangement, for Zainer printed in 1477 a book on chess by Jacopo da Cessole, with vignettes. He was one of the few German printers who employed Roman characters in place of the Gothic of Peter Schoeffer. At Cologne in 1474 Arnold Ther Hoernen published a work entitled *Fasciculus Temporum,* with small illustrations engraved on wood. A Bible without date contains most interesting illustrations. As to the celebrated *Todtentantz,* or "Dance of Death," published about 1485, it contains forty-one relief plates of the most ordinary kind, the same as in the "Chronicle of Cologne" of 1499, of which the figures, though less German, less distorted, are worth little compared with those of the Nuremberg books, more German, but more artistic.

Fig. 19.—The creation of woman, plate from the *Schatzbehalter*, engraved after Michael Wolgemuth.

At Nuremberg, Antony Koburger, called by Badius the prince of booksellers, directed an immense establishment, employing more than a hundred workmen, without counting smaller houses at Basle and Lyons. Koburger was a capable and a fortunate man. He had at first put forth a Bible very indifferently illustrated with the cuts of the Cologne Bible, but he had before him something better than copying others. Michael Wohlgemuth, born at Nuremberg in 1434, was then in the full vigour of his talent. To his school the young Albert Dürer came to study; and as he was able to draw on wood as well as to engrave on copper and paint on panel, Koburger was attracted to him, and engaged him to make a set of illustrations for a book. The projected work was the *Schatzbehalter*, a sort of ascetic compilation, without interest, without arrangement. Michael Wohlgemuth set to work; and, thanks to the ability of his engravers, of whom William Pleydenwurff was probably one, Koburger was able to put the book on sale in the course of 1491 in three hundred and fifty-two folios of two columns. Without being perfection, the designs of Wohlgemuth, very German, very striking, present the vigour and merit of the future school of Nuremberg. The figure is no longer a simple line, in the manner of the block books, but a combination of interlaced cuttings, intended to imitate colour. Those representing the creation of Eve and the daughter of Jephthah are here reproduced. In the search for harmony between the text and engravings of this curious work, we shall find grace and gaiety laid aside, on the other hand a freedom and boldness that interest and permit us to appreciate at their value the Nuremberg artists and Koburger, the printer. In fact, the German artists are more individual, each one taken by himself, than the Italian illustrators could be, condemned as they were to the hierarchical commonplace and to a certain form of idealism into which the art of Italy entered little by little. The German painters, naturalists and believers, presented their heroes in the image of that robust nature that was before their eyes. It was in this rude and unpolished spirit that Michael Wohlgemuth decorated the *Schatzbehalter*; he also composed the designs for the "Nuremberg Chronicle" of Dr. Hartman Schedel, printed by Koburger in 1493.

Fig. 20.—The daughter of Jephthah, plate taken from the *Schatzbehalter* engraved after Michael Wolgemuth.

With Dürer, at the latter end of the fifteenth century, the Book was no more than a pretext for engravings. Thausing, his biographer, says that the great artist felt the necessity of designing an Apocalypse at Rome at the time that Luther was premeditating his religious revolution in face of the worldly splendours of the pontifical court. The "Apocalypse," published in 1511 in Latin, with Gothic characters, was an album of fifteen large wood engravings. The Four Horsemen is the best of these plates, and the boldest; but in this gross fancy, in these poor halting old hacks, the fantastic and grand idea which the artist meant to convey can hardly be seen. It may be said the genius of Dürer was little adapted to vignettes, however large they were, and did not easily lend itself to the exigencies of a spun-out subject. The title of his "Apocalypse" is of its kind a curious example of German genius, but, in spite of its vigour, it does not please like an Italian headpiece or like a French or Flemish frontispiece. The other works of Dürer published in the fifteenth century, "The Life of the Virgin" and "The Passion," were also sets of prints that received a text in the sixteenth century.

Fig. 21.—Title of the "Apocalypse," by Albert Dürer, printed in 1498. First edition, without text.

Stultifera Nauis.

Narragonice pfectionis nunq̃ satis laudata Nauis: per Sebastianū Brant: vernaculo vulgariq; sermone & rhythmo p cūctorȝ mortalium fatuitatis semitas effugere cupiētiū directione/ speculo/ cōmodoq; & salute: proq; inertis ignauęq; stulticię ppetua infamia/ execratione/ & confutatione/ nup fabricata: Atq; iampridem per Iacobum Locher/ cognomēto Philomusum: Sueuū: in latinū traducta eloquiū: & per Sebastianū Brant: denuo seduloq; reuisa: foelici exorditur principio.
·1497·
Nihil sine causa.
Io. de Olpe

Fig. 22.—Title of Sebastian Brandt's "Ship of Fools," printed in 1497 at Basle by Bergman de Olpe.

For the rest of his illustrations Dürer belongs to the sixteenth century, and we shall have occasion to recur to his works. At present it remains to speak of a curious work printed at Basle by Bergman de Olpe in 1497, which appears to be the first comic conception of fifteenth century artists: the *Navis Stultifera*, or "Ship of Fools," of Sebastian Brandt. This work of the school of

Basle lacks neither originality nor vigour. At the time when it was published its success was immense, from the strange tricks of its clowns, with fools' caps, with which every page was adorned. Alas! the best things fall under the satire of these jesters, even the Book and the lover of books, if we may judge by the sarcasms against useless publications volleyed by the personage here reproduced. "I have the first place among fools.... I possess heaps of volumes that I rarely open. If I read them, I forget them, and I am no wiser." Brunet sees in these humorous caricatures more art than is really to be found in them. Their value is owing more to their spirit and humour than to any other artistic merit. Even the engraving is singularly fitted to the subject, with its peculiar cutting, somewhat executed in hairlines. The designer was certainly not a Holbein, but he is no longer the primitive artisan of the first German plates, and his freedom is not displeasing.

Fig. 23.—The *Bibliomaniac*. Engraving from the "Ship of Fools."

We have before spoken, apropos of engraving by the burin in Italy, of the small share of Germany in the essay at illustration by that means, and we do not see a real and serious attempt in the two little coats of arms in copper plate in the *Missale Herbipolense*, printed in 1479.

The Flemish had not taken any great flights in the midst of this almost European movement. The school of Burgundy, whose influence was felt in all the surrounding countries, had lost its authority in consequence of the progress realized at Mayence. Without doubt the great Flemish artists were there, but they were honoured painters, and their inclination did not descend to seeking the booksellers beyond making them offers of service. Besides, the first of these, officially established in Flanders, were two Germans, John of Westphalia and John Veldener, of Cologne, who established themselves in the university of Louvain in 1473, three years after the first Paris printers. John of

Westphalia, who took his own portrait for his mark, edited the *Fasciculus Temporum*, a book which had enormous success in the fifteenth century.

At Haarlem, in spite of the block books attributed to Laurent Coster, illustration was backward. About 1485, a Dutch translation of the *Malheurs de Troye* of Le Fevre was put on sale. This French book was published at Cologne before France possessed the smallest typographical workshop. At Bruges Colard Mansion illuminated the cuts of his *Metamorphoses* of Ovid in 1484. Simple engraving appeared to him far remote from manuscripts of which the vogue had not yet passed away. At Zwoll Peter van Os, the publisher, cut up and used the xylographic plates of the *Biblia Pauperum*, while the master *à la navette*, John of Cologne, an artist in the best sense of the word, was ornamenting certain popular publications with his designs. At Utrecht Veldener came from Louvain to establish a workshop. He published for the second time a *Fasciculus* in 1480; he created a style of decoration with flowers and leaves, which shortly after developed into the trade of *Rahmenschneiders*. Antwerp had attracted Gerard de Leeu from Gouda, and he produced the romance of *Belle Vienne*. Schiedam had an inventive engraver who illustrated an edition of the *Chevalier Delibéré* of Oliver de la Marche, in folio, with Gothic letters, after 1483, as we read in the colophon:—

"Cet traittié fut parfait l'an mil
Quatre cens quatre vings et trois
Ainsi que sur la fin d'avril
Que l'yver est en son exil,
Et que l'esté fait ses explois.
Au bien soit pris en tous endrois
De ceulx à qui il est offert
Par celui qui *Tant a souffert*,
La Marche."

The French language, bright and harmonious, thus found hospitality in other countries. For many examples of French books published abroad, we cannot cite one German work printed in France. Spreading from the north to the south, typography had from 1490 its two principal centres at Paris and Lyons. After the success of the three Germans at the Sorbonne, events took their own course. In 1474 Peter Cæsaris and John Stol, two students who had been instructed by Gering and Krantz, founded the second establishment in Paris, at the sign of the "Soufflet Vert;" and they printed classical works. Ten years later appeared Antony Vérard, Simon Vostre, and Pigouchet, the first of whom gave to French bookselling an impulse that it has not since lost; but before them Pasquier-Bonhomme published his *Grandes Chroniques* in 1476, three volumes folio, the oldest in date of books printed at Paris in French.

The French school of illustration was at its most flourishing point at the end of the fifteenth century, but solely in miniature and ornamentation by the pencil. The charming figures of the manuscripts had at this time a Flemish and naturalistic tendency. The most celebrated of the great artists in manuscripts, John Foucquet, could not deny the source of his talent nor the influence of the Van Eyck school, yet the touch remained distinctly personal. He had travelled, and was not confined to the art circles of a single city, as were so many of the earliest painters of Flanders. He had gone through Italy, and from thence he transported architectural subjects for his curious designs in the *Heures* of Etienne Chevalier, now at Frankfort; a precious fragment of it is preserved in the National Library of Paris. Side by side with this undoubted master, whose works are happily known, lived a more modest artist: John Perréal, called John of Paris, painter to Charles VIII., Louis XII., and Anne of Brittany.

In joining with these two masters, to serve as a transition between Foucquet and Perréal, John Bourdichon, designer to the kings of France from Louis XI. to Francis I., we obtain already a not despicable assemblage of living forces. Without doubt these men were not comparable either with the admirable school of Flanders, or the Germans of Nuremberg, or the masters of Italy; but, moderate as we may deem their merit, they did their tasks day by day, painting miniatures, colouring coats of arms, rendering to the kings, their masters, all the little duties of devoted servants without conceit, and preparing, according to their means, the great artistic movement in France of the seventeenth century. That these men, leaving the brush for the pencil, devoted themselves to design figures on wood, is undeniable. It is said that one of them followed Charles VIII. to the Italian wars, and probably sketched the battles of the campaign as they took place. Now in the books published at this epoch in France we meet with vignettes which so very nearly approach miniatures, that we can easily recognise in them French taste and finish. Such are, for example, the illustrations of the *Mer des Histoires*, printed by Le Rouge in 1488, where suppleness of design is blended in some parts with extraordinary dexterity in engraving. Nevertheless, others leave something to be desired; they maim the best subjects by their unskilful line and their awkwardness of handling. Were not these engravers on wood printers themselves: the Commins, Guyot Marchants, Pierre Lecarrons, Jean

Trepperels, and others? We are tempted to see in certain shapeless work the hasty and light labour of an artisan hurried in its execution. As mentioned above, the part taken by the booksellers in the making of the plates does not make our supposition in itself appear inadmissible.

Printing had been established about twenty years in Paris when Philip Pigouchet, printer and engraver on wood, began to exercise his trade for himself or on account of other publishers. Formerly bookseller in the University, he transported his presses to the Rue de la Harpe, and took for his mark the curious figure here reproduced. At this moment a veritable merchant, Simon Vostre, conceived the idea of putting forth Books of Hours, until then disdained in France, and of publishing them in fine editions with figures, borders, ornaments, large separate plates, and all the resources of typography. The trials made at Venice and Naples between 1473 and 1476 warranted the enterprise. Entering into partnership with Pigouchet, the two were able on the 17th of April, 1488, to place on sale the *Heures à l'Usaige de Rome*, octavo, with varied ornaments and figures. The operation having succeeded beyond their hopes, thanks to the combination of the subjects of the borders, subjects that could be turned and re-turned in all ways so as to obtain the greatest variety, Simon Vostre reapplied himself to the work, and ordered new cuts to augment the number of his decorations. Passavant's idea is commonly received that the engraving was in relief on metal; the line in it is very fine, the background stippled, and the borders without scratches. Wood could not have resisted the force of the press; the reliefs would have been crushed, the borders rubbed and broken. In all the successive editions hard work and wear are not remarked, and we are forced to admit the use of a harder material than the pear or box-wood of ordinary blocks.

Fig. 24.—Mark of Philip Pigouchet, French printer and wood engraver of the fifteenth century.

According to his wants, Simon Vostre designed new series of ornaments. Among them were histories of the saints, Biblical figures, even caricatures against Churchmen, after the manner of the old sculptors, who thought that sin was rendered more horrible in the garb of a monk. Then there were the Dance of Death and sibyls, allying sacred with profane, even the trades, all forming a medley of little figures in the margins, in the borders, nestled among acanthus leaves, distorted men, fantastic animals, and saints piously praying. The Middle Ages live again in these bright and charming books, French in their style, imbued with good sense and perfect toleration.

Fig. 25.—Border in four separate blocks in the *Heures à l'Usaige de Rome*, by Pigouchet, for Simon Vostre, in 1488. Small figures from the "Dance of Death."

The Book rose under Simon Vostre and Philip Pigouchet to the culminating point of ornamentation. Here design and engraving improve and sustain each other. It is not only the stippled backgrounds of the borders that please the eye. And who was this unknown designer, this painter of bold conceptions, whose work is complete in little nothings? However, the large full-page figures have not always an originality of their own, nor the French touch of the borders. Thus that of the Passion here reproduced is inspired line for line by the German, Martin Schongauer. Are we to suppose, that duplicates of blocks passed between France and Germany, or was a copy made by a French designer? It is difficult to say. Still the coincidence is not common to all the missals of the great Parisian bookseller. The Death of the Virgin here reproduced is an evident proof of it. It forms part of the 1488 book, and is a truly French work.

Fig. 26.—Plate copied from Schongauer's Carrying of the Cross, taken from the *Heures* of Simon Vostre.

Fig. 27.—The Death of the Virgin, plate taken from the *Heures* of Simon Vostre, printed in 1488. The border is separate.

It may be said that from the artistic association of Philip Pigouchet and Simon Vostre was born the art of illustration of the Book in France; they worked together for eighteen years, in steady collaboration, and, as far as we know, without a cloud. At Vostre's commencement in 1488 he lived in the Rue Neuve Notre Dame, at the sign of "St. Jean l'Evangeliste;" and in 1520 he was still there, having published more than three hundred editions of the Missal, according to the use of the several cities.

Contemporary with Simon Vostre, another publisher was giving a singular impulse to the Book by his extreme energy, true taste, and the aid of first-class artists. Antony Verard, the most illustrious of the old French booksellers, was a writer, printer, illuminator, and dealer. Born in the second half of the fifteenth century, he established himself in Paris on the Pont Notre Dame, both sides of which were then covered with shops, and about 1485 commenced his fine editions with a "Decameron" in French by Laurent de Premierfait. M. Renouvier remarks in his notice of Verard that his first books were not good, the plates were often unskilful, and were probably borrowed or bought from others; this may be very well understood in a beginner whose modest resources did not permit bold enterprises; the figures were in most cases groundworks for miniatures, outlines and sketches rather than vignettes.

Fig. 28.—Border of the *Grandes Heures* of Antony Verard: Paris, 1498 (?).

Antony Verard was accustomed to take a certain number of fine copies on vellum or paper of each book published by him, in which authorised painters added miniatures and ornaments. It is curious now to find what the cost to one of the great lords of the court of Charles VIII. was of one of these special copies in all the details of its impression, and we find it in a document published by M. Senemaud in a provincial journal (*Bulletin de la Société*

Archéologique de la Charente, 1859, part 2, p. 91), which enables us at the same time to penetrate into a printing office of a great French publisher of the fifteenth century. According to this document, Verard did not disdain to put his own hand to the work, even to carrying the book to the house of his patron if he were a man of consequence. It is an account of Charles de Valois-Angoulême, father of Francis I. He was then living at Cognac; and he ordered Verard to print separately for him on vellum the romance of Tristan, the "Book of Consolation" of Boetius, the *Ordinaire du Chrétien*, and *Heures en François*, each with illuminations and binding. In the detail of expenses Verard omits nothing. He reckons the parchment at three sous four deniers the sheet, the painted and illuminated figures at one écu the large and five sols the small. We give here the outline of one of the plates of the Tristan, ordered by the Duc d'Angoulême, reduced by two-thirds, and from it it may be judged that the profession of the illuminator, even for the time, was by no means brilliant. The binding was in dark-coloured velvet, with two clasps with the arms of the Duke, which cost sixty sous each. The work finished, Verard took the route for Cognac, carrying the precious volumes. He was allowed twenty livres for carriage; and this brings the total to 207 livres 10 sous, equivalent to £200 to £240 of present money.

Fig. 29.—Plate from the Tristan published by Antony Verard, a copy of which was illuminated for Charles of Angoulême.

Verard had preceded Simon Vostre in the publication of books of hours, but his first volume dated 1487 was not successful for the want of borders and frontispieces. At the most he had introduced figures intended for illumination, which, as well as the vignettes, were cut in wood. In 1488, the same year that Simon Vostre commenced his publications, Verard put forth, by "command of the King our lord," the book called the *Grandes Heures*, which is in quarto, Gothic letter, without paging, twenty lines to the full page. This *Grandes Heures* contained fourteen engravings, large borders in four compartments, smaller subjects and initials rubricated by hand. He also published more than two hundred editions between 1487 and 1513, and among them the *Mystère de la Passion*, with eighty figures; the *Grandes Chroniques*, in three folio volumes, printed by John Maurand; the *Bataille Judaïque* of Flavius Josephus; the *Legende Dorée* of Voragine, all books for which he called to his aid rubricators, illuminators, and miniaturists. From the first he had two shops where he put his productions on sale: one on the Pont Notre Dame, the other at the Palace of Justice, "au premier pilier devant la chapelle où l'on chante la messe de messeigneurs les présidents." From 1499, when the Pont Notre Dame was burned, Verard transported his books to the Carrefour St. Severin. At his death in 1513 he was living in the Rue Neuve Notre Dame, "devant Nostre-Dame de Paris."

Besides Verard, Vostre, and Pigouchet, many others will be found who imitated them in the publication of books of hours. The first was John du Pré, who published a Paris missal in 1481, and who was at once printer and bookseller. Like Pigouchet, Du Pré printed books of hours on account of provincial publishers, without dreaming of the competition he was creating for himself. The encroachments of the publishers upon one another, the friendly exchanges, the loans of plates and type, form one of the most curious parts of the study of the Book. Thielman Kerver, a German, also began to put forth books of hours in 1497 in Paris, ornamenting them with borders and figures on wood, and modelling his work completely upon that of Simon Vostre. But after having imitated him, he was associated with him in the publication and sale of the Paris Missal; the competition of these men was evidently an honest one, or the sale of pious works was sufficient to maintain all engaged in it. Established on the Pont St. Michel, at the sign of the "Unicorn," he sold his stock to Gilles Remacle about the beginning of the sixteenth century.

Fig. 30.—Page of the *Grandes Heures* of Antony Verard: Paris, fifteenth century.

Thielman Kerver in his own works shows himself as the rival of Simon Vostre. The Hardouins, who followed the same profession, do not appear to have attained the success of their predecessors; and, excepting in the *Heures à l'Usage de Rome*, published in 1503 by Gilles Hardouin on the Pont au Change, at the sign of the "Rose," they servilely imitated them. There was also among the disciples of Vostre William Eustache, bookseller to the King, "tenant la boutique dedans la grant salle du palais du costé de messeigneurs les présidens, ou sur les grans degrés du costé de la conciergerie à l'ymage St. Jean levangeliste." Eustache made use of the work of Pigouchet and Kerver, not to mention the printers of the end of the fifteenth century.

We have named the principal, the fortunate ones; but what becomes of the crowd of other publishers whose hopes vanished before the success of Vostre and Verard? There were Denis Meslier, with his quarto *Heures de Bourges*, and Vincent Commin, bookseller of the Rue Neuve Notre Dame, who thus appealed to his customers:—

"Qui veult en avoir? On en treuve
A tres grand marché et bon pris
A la Rose, dans la rue Neuve
De Nostre-Dame de Paris."

There were also Robin Chaillot, Laurent Philippe, and a hundred others whose names have died with them or are only preserved on the torn pages of their works.

Fig. 31.—Plate from a book of hours of Simon Vostre, representing the massacre of the Innocents.

But if books of this kind found vogue and a large sale at this epoch, the dealers did not keep to pious publications only. By a singular mixture of the sacred and the profane, the bookmen put on sale on their stalls the "Decameron" of Boccaccio as well as the "Hours of the Immaculate Virgin," and the purchasers thought fit to make the acquaintance of the one as well as the other. Besides, the end of the fifteenth century had its literary preferences, its alluring titles, its attractive frontispieces. At the commencement of the present century double titles—"Atala; or, The Child of Mystery;" "Waverley; or, Sixty Years Since"—were common, although now out of fashion. Since then came books of travels—*Voyages au Pays des Milliards*, etc. In the fifteenth century, and even since the fourteenth, a series of titles was in public favour. There was first the *Débats*, or "Dialogues:" *Débat de la Dame et de l'Escuyer*, Paris, 1490, folio; "Dialogue of Dives and Pauper," London, Richard Pynson, 1493; and many other eccentric titles. There came also thousands of *complaintes*, a kind of lay in verse or prose; *blasons*, light pieces describing this or that thing; *doctrinals*, that had nothing to do with doctrine. And among the most approved subjects, between the piety of some and the gaiety of others, the Dances of Death established themselves firmly, showing, according to the hierarchy of classes then prevalent, Death taking the great ones of the earth, torturing equally pope, emperor, constable, or minstrel, grimacing before youth, majesty, and love. Long before printing appeared, the

Dances of Death took the lead; they were some consolation for the wretched against their powerful masters, the revenge of the rabble against the king; they may be seen painted, sculptured, illuminated, when engraving was not there to multiply their use; they may be seen largely displayed on walls, sombre, frightful, at Dresden, Leipzig, Erfurt, Berne, Lucerne, Rouen, Amiens, and Chaise-Dieu. It was the great human equality, attempted first by the French, then by the inimitable Holbein.

Fig. 32.—Dance of Death, said to be by Verard. The Pope and the Emperor.

Fig. 33.—Dance of Death of Guyot Marchant in 1486. The Pope and the Emperor.

We can imagine the impression these bitter ironies made on the oppressed and disdained lower classes. The first "Dance of Death" was produced by Guyot Marchant in 1485, in ten leaves and seventeen engravings, in folio, with Gothic characters. Marchant describes himself as "demeurant en Champ Gaillart à Paris le vingt-huitiesme jour de septembre mil quatre cent quatre-vingtz et cinq." The book must have gone off rapidly, for it was republished in the following year, with additions and new engravings. French illustration was already moving forward, as may be judged by the reproductions here given from the folio edition of 1486. Pope and emperor, glory and power, are led and plagued by Death, hideous Death, with open body and frightful grin.

We could wish that the tendencies and processes of what may be called the second generation of printers were well understood. In a few years they surmounted the difficulties of their art, and made the Book a model of elegance and simplicity. The smallest details were cared for, and things apparently the most insignificant were studied and rendered practical.

Speaking of titles, an enormous progress was here made in the publications of the end of the century. In Italy the subjects of decoration ordinarily formed a framework for the front page, wherein were included useful indications. The most ancient specimen of this kind has already been referred to. A model of this species is the "St. Jerome," published at Ferrara by Lorenzo Rossi, of Valenza, in 1497, folio; the title, much adorned, is in Gothic letters; the engraved initial is very adroitly left in outline, so as not to burden or break the text.

In Germany there was already the appearance of bad taste and prodigality, the letters crossing each other, the Gothic type covered with bizarre appendices, the titles intricate; later they became illegible even for the Germans.

Fig. 34.—Typographical mark of Thielman Kerver.

In France the first page gave the most circumstantial indications of the contents of the work, the name and abode of the printer and bookseller. Often these titles were ornamented with movable frameworks, printed in Gothic, sometimes in two colours, which necessitated two printings, one for the black and one for the red ink. The mark of the printer or publisher generally appeared, and it was nearly always a charming work. These French marks were all more or less treated heraldically; that is to say, the initials occupy a shield, sustained by supporters and cut with extreme care. The first was that of Fust and Schoeffer at Mayence, of admirable simplicity and grace. In France this early specimen of the trade mark took with Simon Vostre and Verard the shape of delicate illustrations, finely designed and carefully engraved; but the custom of allusive marks did not prevail, as we shall have occasion to see, until the sixteenth century. The mark of Pigouchet has already been given; that of Thielman Kerver is conceived in the same principles of taste and art. The sign of his house being the "Unicorn," Kerver took as supporters to his shield two unicorns *affrontées*.

In these colophons are found philosophic aphorisms, satirical remarks, marvels of poetry. A certain bookseller paid court to the powerful university, which dispensed glory and riches to the poor tradesmen by buying many books. Andrew Bocard engraved on his mark this flattery as a border:—

"Honneur au Roy et à la court,
Salut à l'université
Dont nostre bien procède et sourt.
Dieu gart de Paris la cité!"

The Germans introduced into their colophons some vainglorious notices. Arnold Ther Hoernen, already mentioned, who printed the *Theutonista* at Cologne in 1477, boasted in it of having corrected it all with his own hands. Jean Treschel, established at Lyons in 1493, proclaims himself a German, because the Germans were the inventors of an art that he himself possessed to an eminent degree. He prided himself on being what we may call a skilled typographer; "virum hujus artis solertissimum," he writes without false modesty. At times, in the colophons of his books, he attempted Latin verse, the Sapphic verse of Horace, of a playful turn, to say that his work was perfected in 1494.

"Arte et expensis vigilique cura
Treschel explevit opus hoc Joannes,
Mille quingentos ubi Christus annos
Sex minus egit.
Jamque Lugduni juvenes, senesque,
Martias nonas celebres agebant
Magna Reginæ quia prepotenti
Festa parabant."

Fig. 35.—Frontispiece to Terence, published by Treschel at Lyons in 1493. The author writing his book.

The portrait is another element of illustration, the figure of the author prefixed to his work. It had already been a custom in the manuscripts to paint on the first leaf of the work the likeness of him who composed it, frequently in the act of presenting his book to some noble patron; and in this way is often preserved the only known portrait of either patron or author. Printing and engraving rendered these effigies more common, the portraits of one often served for another, and the booksellers used them without very much scruple. As we shall see later, this became in the sixteenth century a means of illustrating a book plainly, but only at the time when the portrait, drawn or painted, commenced to be more widely used. Previously the *clichés* of which we speak went everywhere, from the Italians to the French, from Æsop to Accursius; these uncertain physiognomies began with the manuscript romances of chivalry, from whence they were servilely copied in typography. From the first the Italians mixed the ancient and the modern. Thus in a *Breviarium*, printed in 1478, there is an engraved portrait of Paul Florentin. On the same principle, the portrait of Burchiello, an early Italian poet, was later reproduced in England as a likeness of William Caxton.

In France the author is often represented writing, and it was so up to the middle of the sixteenth century. In an edition of *Des Cas des Nobles Hommes*, by Jean Dupré, in 1483, Boccaccio is represented seated, having before him his French translator, Laurent de Premierfait. This plate is one of the oldest representations of authors in French books. In the *Roman de la Rose*, first edition of Paris and Lyons, in folio, probably published by William Leroy about 1485, William de Lorris, the author, is shown in his bed:—

"Une nuyt comme je songeoye,
Et de fait dormir me convient,
En dormant un songe m'advint...."

Fig. 36.—Woodcut from Caxton's "Game and Playe of the Chesse."

There is also a portrait of Alain Chartier in his *Faits*, printed in 1489. In the Terence of Treschel, of Lyons, in 1493, we see a grammarian of the fifteenth century in a furnished room of the time occupied in writing at a desk; this is Guy Jouvenal, of Mans, the author of the commentary.

Fig. 37.—The Knight, a woodcut from Caxton's "Game and Playe of the Chesse."

While this good work was progressing so nobly in France, Italy, and Germany, the typographers of England were by no means idle, although the illustration of the Book in the fifteenth century was not there so forward. William Caxton had produced over sixty works, the colophons of many of them revealing much of the personal life and character of the first English printer. Some of them were ornamented with woodcuts; we reproduce two from the "Game and Playe of the Chesse," printed in folio, about 1476. The first represents a king and another person playing at chess; the smaller cut is a representation of the knight, who is thus described in Caxton's own words: "The knyght ought to be maad al armed upon an hors in suche wise that he have an helme on his heed and a spere in his right hond, and coverid with his shelde, a swerde and a mace on his left syde, clad with an halberke and plates tofore his breste, legge harnoys on his legges, spores on his heelis, on hys handes hys gauntelettes, hys hors wel broken and taught, and apte to bataylle, and coveryd with hys armes." The other Caxton block which we reproduce is a representation of music from the "Mirrour of the World," a thin folio volume of one hundred leaves printed in 1481, with thirty-eight woodcuts. These specimens will serve to show the rudimentary character of English wood engraving in the fifteenth century. No authentic portrait of Caxton is known, and the one that is generally accepted is really a portrait of an Italian poet, Burchiello, taken from an octavo edition of his work on Tuscan poetry, printed 1554; this was copied by Faithorne for Sir Hans Sloane as the portrait of Caxton, and was reproduced by Ames in his "Typographical Antiquities," 1749. Lewis prefixed the portrait here given to his "Life of Mayster Willyam Caxton," 1737, which is a copy of Faithorne's drawing with some alterations. John Lettou and William Machlinia issued various statutes and other legal works.

Fig. 38.—Music, a woodcut from Caxton's "Mirrour of the World."

Fig. 39.—William Caxton, from Rev. J. Lewis' "Life."

Wynken de Worde continued printing up to 1534, and issued over four hundred works. He used no less than nine different marks, all of them bearing Caxton's initials, evidencing the regard of the pupil for his master; the mark which we reproduce is one of rare occurrence. Richard Pynson began in 1493, and continued well into the sixteenth century, and was one of the first of the "privileged" printers, authorised to issue the legal and parliamentary publications. One of the marks used by him is here reproduced. Julian Notary began in 1498. The only style of illustration used by any of these early printers was the woodcut, and of this there was very little beyond the title-page and printer's mark. The artistic form of the Book originated on the Continent, but England was not slow to adopt it and fashion it to her own ends.

Fig. 40.—Mark of Wynken de Worde.

Fig. 41.—Mark of Richard Pynson.

Thus was printing spread abroad, carrying with it to the countries where it was established the rules of an unchangeable principle; but, according to its surroundings, it was so transformed in a few years that its origin was no longer recognised. It was light in Italy, heavy in Germany, gay in France. Painting, of which it was accidentally the issue, returned to it under the form of illustration a short time after its first and fruitful essays. The Gothic character, generally used in Germany, continued in France with the Vostres, the Verards, and others up to the middle of the sixteenth century, although the first artisans before this used Roman type; it was also the prevailing type used in English books. In Italy it was Jenson, a Frenchman, who gave to the matrix the alphabet preserved to the present time; and it was the Venetians and Florentines who learned before all others the art of judicious ornamentation of the Book. The French came very near perfection, thanks to their printers and booksellers, at the end of the century; and the Germans found illustrious artists to scatter their compositions in their large, heavy works.

CHAPTER III.

1500 TO 1600.

French epics and the Renaissance—Venice and Aldus Manutius—Italian illustrators—The Germans: *Theuerdanck*, Schäufelein—The Book in other countries—French books at the beginning of the century, before the accession of Francis I.—Geoffroy Tory and his works—Francis I. and the Book—Robert Estienne—Lyons a centre of bookselling; Holbein's Dances of Death—School of Basle—Alciati's emblems and the illustrated books of the middle of the century—The school of Fontainebleau and its influence—Solomon Bernard—Cornelis de la Haye and the *Promptuaire*—John Cousin—Copper plate engraving and metal plates—Woériot—The portrait in the Book of the sixteenth century—How a book was illustrated on wood at the end of the century—Influence of Plantin on the Book; his school of engravers—General considerations—Progress in England—Coverdale's Bible—English printers and their work—Engraved plates in English books

OUR simple division into chapters will be understood without difficulty as not corresponding exactly with the most momentous epochs in the history of the Book in France and abroad. Doubtless it would be easy for France alone to find some limits and to furnish scholastic formulæ by which contemporary publishers might be grouped. But in order to present, as in a synoptical table, an essential and abridged sketch of the Book in all European countries, it appeared to us more convenient to begin with the confused and tangled notions by centuries and to unfold in our review the characteristic facts of each country conjointly. Moreover, after the sixteenth century neither Italy nor Germany could compare with France, which, less fortunate, perhaps, at the beginning than her neighbours, surpassed them in all the pride of her genius.

The commencement of the sixteenth century found the French army in Italy, under the command of Louis XII. Marching from glory to glory, the French successively saw Pisa, Capua, and Naples, and that which has since been called the Renaissance displayed itself little by little to the conquerors. At Venice was living Aldus Pius Manutius, then the greatest printer of the entire world. Aldus was proprietor of the celebrated printing office of Nicholas Jenson, through his father-in-law, Andrea Torresani, of Asola, who acquired it on the death of the French printer; and he had in a few years reached a position in which he was without a rival. We have seen that he composed, at the end of the fifteenth century, the admirable volume *Hypnerotomachia*, the renown of which became universal. Aldus was fifty-two years of age, having been born in 1447; and his learning was increased by daily intercourse with learned Italians, among them the celebrated Pico de la Mirandola. His establishment at Venice in 1488 had for its object the creation of a chair in Greek, in which language he was well instructed from his youth. Occupied with the idea of issuing editions of the principal Greek writers, which up to then remained in manuscript, he engaged himself in the formation of a printing office. He first published the *Herone et Leandro* of Musæus in 1494, quarto, in a Greek character apparently designed by him, and perhaps engraved by Francisco da Bologna; then the Greek grammar of Constantine Lascaris, with the date of 1494; and the works of Aristotle in five folio volumes. At the time of the Italian wars Aldus was making a revolution in typography, by producing more practical sizes and finer characters, which would permit a volume of the smallest height to contain the matter of a folio printed with large type. Legend says that the new letters were copied exactly from the handwriting of Petrarch, inclining like all cursive writing; the name of *Italic* was given to this character, which was also called *Aldine*, from its inventor. It was engraved by Francisco da Bologna. Aldus published in octavo size, with this kind of letter, an edition of Virgil in 1501, then a Horace, a Juvenal, a Martial, and a Petrarch in the same year. The following year, 1502, he gave an edition of the *Terze Rime* of Dante, and for the first time took as his typographical mark an anchor encircled by a dolphin.[3]

[3] Tory in his *Champfleury* explains thus the mark of Aldus and his device, which was in Greek the "Make haste slowly" of Boileau: "The anchor signifies tardiness, and the dolphin haste, which is to say that in his business he was moderate."

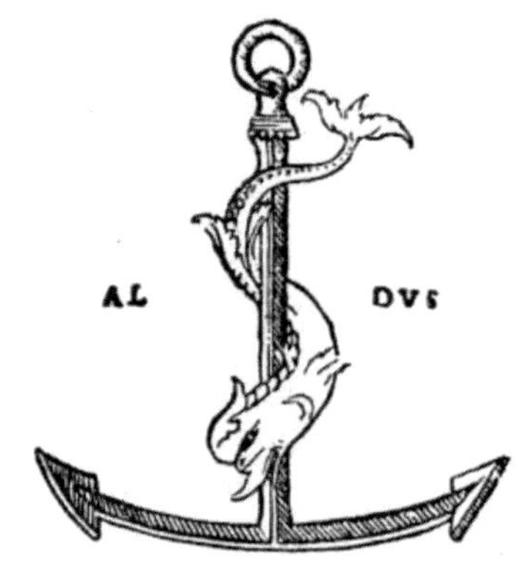

Fig. 42.—The anchor and dolphin, mark of Aldus Manutius, after the original in the *Terze Rime* of 1502, where it appears for the first time.

His marriage with the daughter of Andrea Torresani, of Asola, brought together into his possession two printing houses. The burden became too heavy for Manutius to think henceforth of publishing by himself. Besides, the wars did not allow him any repose, of which he bitterly complained in his prefaces. He attracted learned Greek scholars, who supervised, each one in his specialty, the works in progress, and founded a society, an Aldine academy, in which the greatest names of the epoch were united. Aldus conveys the perfect idea of a great printer of those times, doing honour to celebrated men, in spite of business preoccupations and of the annoyance caused by the war. It is said that Erasmus, passing through Venice, called on him, and not making himself known, was badly received by the powerful printer. All at once, at the name of the distinguished visitor, Aldus, overwhelmed for an instant, rose in great haste and showed him how highly he appreciated men of letters.

The war finished by ruining this state of affairs. In 1505 Aldus quitted Venice to travel, and on his return found it poorer than when he went away. Andrea d'Asola, his father-in-law, came to his aid; but the great printer had received his death-blow; and in spite of the activity which he brought to the new establishment, he further declined until 1515, when he expired, leaving an inextricable confusion to his son Paul.

He had early abandoned illustration for the scientific and useful in his publications; besides, the size of book chosen by him did not admit of plates; but other publishers employed artists in the ornamentation of the Book. Lucantonio Giunta, the most celebrated among them, was printer and engraver, a striking example of the affinity of the two trades from their origin. In 1508 Lucantonio Zonta, as he then spelt his name, published a Roman breviary in large quarto, with twelve engravings in the Lombardo-Venetian manner, signed "L. A.," in very good style. The same artist-publisher cut a portrait of Virgil for an edition of that poet about 1515. Furthermore, Giunta did not alone illustrate the book from his own office. Other designers lent him their assistance. We find evidence of this in the Bible printed by him in 1519 in small octavo.

Fig. 43.—Mark of Lucantonio Giunta, of Venice.

The most meritorious of the artists of Venice at this time was John Andrea, known as Guadagnino. He designed the vignettes for Florus's epitome of Livy, printed at Venice for Melchior Sessa and Peter of Ravenna (1520, folio); in 1516 he copied the plates of Dürer's *Apocalypse* for that of Alexander Paganini, of Venice. A Venetian work which signalised the beginning of the sixteenth century was the *Trionfo di Fortuna* of Sigismond Fanti, of Ferrara, printed by Agostino da Portese in 1527.

Venice was the home of Titian, and at the present time the great artist was at the height of his glory. In 1518 two brothers, Nicholas and Dominic dal Gesù, published a translation of the celebrated "Golden Legend" of Voragine. The plates which were added to the work were manifestly inspired by the school of the Venetian master. Unhappily the engravers have not always equalled the genius of the drawings.

To resume, the city of Venice was, at the beginning of the sixteenth century, one of the most prolific in publishers and artists of talent. Since the first establishments of the Germans, typography had successively employed in Venice Nicholas Jenson, a Frenchman, inventor of the Roman character; Erhard Ratdolt, the first to employ illustration there; and Aldus Manutius, scholar and printer, whose progress in printing elevated that art to the highest rank among human discoveries; there were also remarkable engravers and draughtsmen, among others Guadagnino and Giunta, besides the anonymous masters of the school of Titian. The part of Venice in the movement, then, was great, but it may be explained by the riches of its citizens, the extent of its commerce, and the genius it possessed.

If we now return from Venice to the north, to Milan, the school of Leonardo da Vinci will make itself apparent in the Book. In order of date we will mention the *Mysterii Gesta Beatæ Veronicæ Virginis*, published by Gotardo de Ponte 1518, small quarto, with figures in the style of Luini, and Vitruvius in Italian by Cesariano. On the testimony of the author, the wood engravings in a book of Fra Luca Pacioli, *De Divina Proportione*, are attributed to Leonardo da Vinci. M. Delaborde does not believe this, but M. Passavant does.

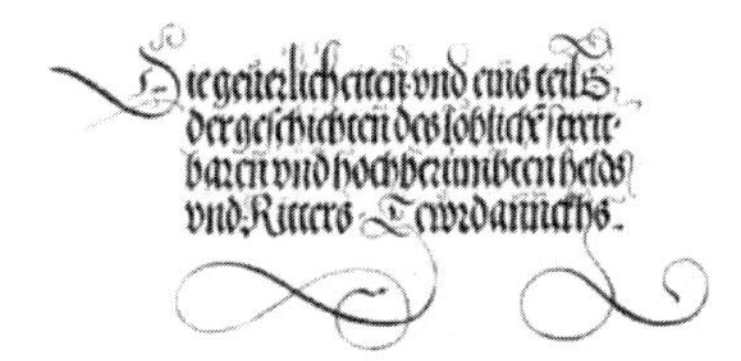
Die geuerlicheiten vnd eins teils
der geschichten des loblichē streit-
baren vnd hochberümbten helds
vnd Ritters Tewrdannckhs.

Fig. 44.—Title of the *Theuerdanck*. The flourishes of the letters are printed.

In Germany, Nuremberg continued, with Albert Dürer and the artists of his school, to furnish book illustrations at the beginning of the century. The master reprinted his valuable engravings of the "Life of the Virgin" in 1511, and also the "Apocalypse." But after him the art commenced to decline; a hundred years later nothing remained of the honour and glory gained by Germany in the commencement. Among the most interesting of the Nuremberg publications is a chivalric poem by Melchior Pfinzfing, composed for the marriage of Maximilian and Mary of Burgundy. As M. Delaborde in his *Débuts de l'Imprimerie* well remarks, this is not a book destined for sale by a bookseller; it is a work of art destined by an emperor for his friends, and he saw that it was an unapproachable work.

Fig. 45.—Plate taken from the *Theuerdanck*, representing Maximilian and Mary of Burgundy. Engraved on wood after Schäufelein.

Bold strokes, majestic letters, intertwined ornaments, are here multiplied. Three persons worked upon it for five years; these were, Peutinger says, Hans Leonard Schäufelein, the painter, Jost Necker, the engraver, and Schönsperger, the printer of Augsburg, who quitted his native city for Nuremberg. When they were able to take a proof, craftsmen were unwilling to believe it to be a book composed in movable characters; they were sure, on the contrary, that it was a true xylograph, cut in wood; and, in fact, from the title here reproduced, the error was excusable. This work, which is now called the *Theuerdanck*, from the name of the hero of the romance, is ornamented with a number of wood engravings, numbered by Arabic figures. We reproduce one of the last plates, in which Theuerdanck—Maximilian—is introduced to the Queen—Mary of Burgundy. The designs of Schäufelein recall very nearly the work of Albert Dürer, his master; but, as we said of him, these works, heavy and dull, although very clever, do not always suit as vignettes. Again, our criticism does not extend so much to the *Theuerdanck*, whose letters, excessively ornamented and much flattened, furnish a framework more suitable for the engravings than would a more slender character, which would be completely overshadowed by the German plate.

When we have mentioned the *Passional Christi* of Lucas Cranach, published by J. Grünenberg at Wittemberg in 1521—twenty-six mediocre wood engravings—we shall have cited the most important of the interesting and rare volumes published in Germany at the commencement of the sixteenth century.

The Netherlands, Spain, and England were working, but without great success. In the Low Countries Plantin and his gigantic enterprises may be recalled. In Spain the taste had not yet developed itself; and although the drawing of illustrations may be careful enough, the wood-cutting is pitiable. We will mention the Seneca of Toledo in 1510, and the "Chronicle of Aragon" in 1523. Of England we will speak later.

In France, on the contrary, we find an enormous commerce in books at the commencement of the sixteenth century. All the publishers mentioned in the preceding chapter were still living, and they were feeling the effects of the French conquests in Italy. The dithyrambic literature then inaugurated, and which had its origin under Louis XII., exercised a bad influence equally upon the printers and decorators of the Book. Doubtless the composition of the text and engravings was done hastily, for the great people did not like to wait for this kind of history. *Le Vergier d'Honneur*, written by Octavian de St. Gelais and Andry de la Vigne, was thus published about the end of the fifteenth century and ornamented with hasty vignettes, probably at the expense of Antoine Verard. Upon the accession to the throne of Louis XII., Claude de

Seyssel, his master of council, composed *Les Louenges du Roy Louis XII.*, and soon after translated it from Latin into French for the same Verard, who printed it in 1508.

The taste for historical works induced the publishers to produce *La Mer des Histoires*, which had already been published in the fifteenth century; Thielman Kerver put forth the "Compendium" of Robert Gaguin in 1500 on account of Durand Gerlier and John Petit. The French version of this work was given in 1514 by Galliot du Pré, with vignettes, and afterwards under the name of *Mirouer Historial*, by Renaud Chaudière in 1520, by Nyverd, and others; the same with the *Rozier Historial*, with figures, in 1522 and 1528. Among the most popular works was the *Illustrations de la Gaule et Singularitez de Troye*, by John le Maire de Belges, printed in Paris and ornamented. In 1512 it was published by Geoffroy de Marnef, in 1515 by John and Gilbert de Marnef, by Regnault, by Philip le Noir, and others, always in the Gothic characters which prevailed in France at the beginning of the sixteenth century.

We give from the curious book of John le Maire an interesting woodcut representing Queen Anne of Brittany as Juno, in which we can without much difficulty see a remarkable sketch by a Bourdichon or a Perréal. The truly French style of this figure leaves no doubt as to its origin. At the same time, it may possibly have been inspired by the Virgin of a German master, say one of 1466, judging from the accessories, and even from the pose. This engraving will be found in the edition of 1512 of Gilbert de Marnef, in Gothic letter, quarto. On the reverse are the arms and device of John le Maire de Belges.

The time that elapsed from the death of Louis XI. until the accession of Francis I.—that is to say, from 1483 to 1515—was, to employ an old expression, the golden age of French printing and illustration. Under Charles VIII. and Louis XII. the designers on wood were not yet affected by the neighbouring schools; neither the accentuated Italian influence nor the German processes had reached them; they did in their own way that which came to them, and they did it in their own fashion and habit, without foreign influence. Further, the kings did not ignore them, and Louis XII. preserved to the printers of the university all their rights and privileges in a magniloquent ordinance, in which the art of typography was extolled in the highest terms. It restores to them all the advantages that they had lost. It recites, "In consideration of the great benefit that has come to our kingdom by means of the art and science of printing, the invention of which seems more Divine than human, which, thanks to God, has been invented and found in our time by the help and industry of booksellers, by which our holy Catholic faith has been greatly augmented and strengthened, justice better understood and administered, and Divine service more honourably and diligently made, said, and celebrated, ... by means of which our kingdom precedes all others," etc., etc. (Blois, 9th April, 1513). Certainly Louis made the best of himself and his kingdom in this preamble, but it must be recognised that France already held a predominant rank in the new industry, and that beyond the Italians she had no fear of serious rivalry. The school of ornamentists made constant progress. Before the books of hours, the booksellers contented themselves with miserable blocks, placed side by side, forming a framework of good and bad together; but after Simon Vostre, Verard, and the others they were singularly refined. The borders, at least in the books of hours, had become the principal part of the book; they had in them flowers, architectural, complicated, and simple subjects, all of perfect taste and extreme elegance; and, as we have observed in the representation of Anne of Brittany in the *Illustrations de la Gaule*, the figure subjects were no longer mechanical, commonplace, and tiresome blocks, but, on the contrary, more often works specially designed and engraved by artists of merit.

Fig. 46.—Vignette taken from the *Illustrations de la Gaule et Singularitez de Troye*. Queen Anne of Brittany as Juno.

Lentree de la Royne en sa ville
& Cite de Paris. Imprimee
par le Commãdemẽt du Roy
nostre Sire.

On la vend a Paris en la Rue Sainct Iac-
ques deuant Lescu De Basle, & deuant
Leglise de la Magdaleine, A Lenseigne
du Pot Casse. Auec Priuilege.

Fig. 47.—Title of the *Entree d'Eléonore d'Autriche a Paris*, by Guillaume Bochetel. Printed by Geoffroy Tory in May, 1531, quarto.

Geoffroy Tory, born at Bourges in 1480, continued after Vostre and Verard the onward march of illustration of the Book. He was a sort of encyclopædist, who knew and foresaw everything, but with a singularly subtler and finer genius than his predecessors. There is now very little doubt that at first Tory was an engraver and printer. Moreover, he published with Jean Petit one of his first volumes, the geography of Pomponius Mela, printed by Gilles de Gourmont in 1507. Tory was then an erudite and diffusive commentator. Later he published a book with poor engravings (*Valerii Probi Grammatici Opusculum*, 1510), waiting until his good star should place him on the right road. He had for his mark, say the bibliographers, the cross of Lorraine (†), small enough to be lost in the ornamentation of his plates. Really this sign is found in Tory's mark—the "Pot Cassé"—the broken jar—and also sometimes in the letter G, which was his ordinary signature. This opinion, which we will not try to contradict in a popular work like this, appears to us to err, as others used this mark, as may be judged from the essentially different touches of engravings bearing the cross of Lorraine, and particularly those of Woériot in the middle of the century.

If M. A. Bernard[4] may be credited, Geoffroy Tory cultivated all the sciences with equal success. For our purpose, suffice it to recognise his right to one of the first places in the art of decoration of books of hours. Doubtless his travels in Italy had contributed to modify his taste and to detach him a little from the sober and simple manner that then characterised French engraving; but he nevertheless preserved the indelible traces of the origin of his art, in the same way as some people cannot correct their provincial accent. The *Heures de la Vierge*, which he designed, and which he had engraved about 1520, on account of Simon de Colines, is marvellously surrounded by ornaments, until then unknown in France; at the same time, and in spite of other tendencies, it is purely a French work, and the specimen given here is a convincing proof.

[4] *Geoffroy Tory, Peintre et Graveur, Premier Imprimeur Royal, Réformateur de l'Orthographe et de la Typographie*: Paris, 1857, 8vo.

Domine, ne in furore
tuo arguas me: neq;
in ira tua corripias
me.
Miſerere mei domi-
ne, quoniã infirmus
ſum: ſana me domine, quoniam con-
turbata ſunt oſſa mea.
Et anima mea turbata eſt valde: ſed
tu domine vſquequo?
Conuertere domine, & eripe animam
meam: ſaluum me fac propter miſe-
ricordiam tuam.
Quoniam non eſt in morte, qui me-
mor ſit tui: in inferno autẽ, quis con-
fitebitur tibi?
Laboraui in gemitu meo, lauabo per
ſingulas noctes lectũ meum, lachry-
mis meis ſtratum meum rigabo.
Turbatus eſt à furore oculus meus.

Fig. 48.—Full page of the *Heures* of Simon de Colines, by Tory.

Fig. 49.—*Heures* of Geoffroy Tory. The Circumcision.

Fig. 50.—*Heures* of Simon de Colines, with the mark of the Cross of Lorraine.

Geoffroy Tory composed a curious book, as poetic as learned, in which he studied at once the form of the letter from the typographic and the emblematic point of view, and also the French orthography of the time. He tells us himself that he was brought to commence this book on the fête-day of the kings,

1523, when, after a frugal repast, he was, he says, "dreaming on my bed and revolving my memory, thinking of a thousand little fancies, serious and mirthful, among which I thought of some antique letters that I had made for Monseigneur the treasurer for war, Master Jehan Grolier, councillor and secretary of our lord the King, amateur of fine letters and of all learned personages." Tory called his book *Champfleury, auquel est contenu l'art et science de la deue proportion des lettres ... selon le corps et le visage humain*, and he published it himself in small folio, putting upon it the sign of Gilles de Gourmont, in 1529.

At heart Tory had been fascinated by the theories of Dürer on the proportions of the human body; and he says, "The noble German painter Albert Dürer is greatly to be praised that he has so well brought to light his art of painting in designing geometrical forms, the ramparts of war, and the proportions of the human body." He wished to indicate the true measure of letters to his contemporaries, "the number of points and turns of the compass that each one requires." The most amusing part of this curious treatise is his short academical preface, where, under a playful form, the great publisher studies the orthography of his time, and exclaims against the forgers of new words, the Latinisers of the language, "the skimmers of Latin, jesters and gibberers, ... who mock not only their shadows, but themselves." The entire passage was copied by Rabelais, nearly literally, and it indicates that its author was possessed of good sense, which, unhappily, all his contemporaries were not.

For the technical part, he added to his theories a number of designs of geometrical letters, but he was carried away, after the fashion of the time, by Greek and Roman models, perhaps a little further than he meant, losing himself in the midst of idle dissertations. To these geometrical engravings he added small and charming figures, said to be by Jean Perréal, as well as emblematical letters of the nature of the Y which is here given, with explanatory text and commentary. To him this Y had two branches: one of virtue and one of vice; that of virtue shows palms, crowns, a sceptre, and a book; that of vice birches, a gallows, and fire.

Fig. 51.—Emblematical letter Y, taken from the *Champfleury* of Geoffroy Tory.

With the importance that cannot be denied to his works, Geoffroy Tory founded a school; and it was from his workshop that the plates came for the book of Paulus Jovius on the dukes of Milan, published by Robert Estienne in 1549, quarto. The portraits of the dukes in this work have been attributed to Tory himself, but he died in 1533, and there is not the least indication that he engraved these sixteen portraits with his own hand sixteen years before their publication. Besides, our doubts as to the cross of Lorraine being the exclusive signature of Tory, as has been believed, lead us to think it the collective mark of a workshop, as we meet it on works long after the death of the master. As a proof, the mark is found on the engravings of *L'Entrée du Roi à Paris* in 1549, which cannot be taken as a posthumous work of Tory, for these engravings had their origin at a certain and special date. But in spite of the absence of the monogram, the admirable block from the Diodorus Siculus of Antoine Macault might, from its design and engraving, be considered as by Tory himself. Holbein, who, about the same time, designed a somewhat similar scene, the King of France seated on a throne receiving poison from the hands of Death, never did anything better. Within the scanty proportions of the design, all the figures are portraits. Duprat, Montmorency and the three sons of the King may be recognised; Macault, on the left, is reading his translation to a circle of nobles and men of letters. This admirable page is one of the truest and most skilful of the monuments of French engraving; it is equal to the best inventions of Holbein, and it marks the culminating point of the illustration of the Book before the exaggerations of the school of Fontainebleau. Geoffroy Tory was not the publisher. The Diodorus Siculus, doubtless prepared two or three years before, was not published until 1535, in quarto, with his ordinary mark of the "Pot Cassé."

Fig. 52.—Macault reading to Francis I. his translation of Diodorus Siculus. Wood engraving attributed to Tory.

We have now arrived through him at the reign of Francis I., who was called the father of letters, and who for various reasons favoured the arts. Doubtless grand paintings and the decoration of the royal palaces interested him more than vignettes in books and the efforts of printers; but, at the same time, books occupied him. He studied much, and in his travels accumulated many volumes. An account in the French National Archives shows that Claude Chappuis, his librarian, packed entire cases, which were sent to Dauphiné at the time of the wars of Piedmont, the carriage costing twenty livres tournois. Francis had, moreover, following sudden impulses, curious fits of wantonness and mischief. It was perceived a little later that the doctrines of Luther were propagated by the Book; and the Sorbonne was up in arms, on the pretence of imposing its own expurgated text of the Bible on the publishers and tolerating no other. Theodore Beza, enemy of the Sorbonnists, said with regard to this (we translate the antique French literally), "Our great doctors with cherubic visage have forbidden men to see the Holy Bible in vulgar language, of which every one has knowledge, because, they say, the desire of knowing everything engenders nothing but error, fear, and care. *Arguo sic*, if they so, for its abuse, wish to take away this book, it is clear also that it is their duty to put away the wine with which each of them makes himself drunk."

Fig. 53.—Robert Estienne, after the engraving in the *Chronologie Collée*.

This piece is only cited to show to what lengths matters had gone, thanks to printing. It is very certain that all the pamphlets, placards, and other horrors published to raise religious warfare, did not aid in the progress of the Book. The King was not always disinterested on the technical question; books merited encouragement, at least as much as castigation, and besides, as time passed, they gradually transformed men and ideas. In spite of apparent severities, was not the King himself a little touched by contact with the new religion, like his sister Marguerite, or his sister-in-law, Renée of Ferrara? However that may be, he twice showed himself a resolute partisan of the celebrated Robert Estienne, son-in-law and associate of Simon de Colines, whose works in point of erudition and typography assumed day by day more importance. Robert Estienne had the great honour of being chosen from all his contemporaries by King Francis as the royal printer. This prince had ordered to be engraved for him by Claude Garamond, after the design of Ange Vergèce, the first cutter of matrices of his time, a special Greek character in three sizes, which was used in 1544 to compose the "Ecclesiastical History" of Eusebius. These are the famous royal types—*typi regii*—as Estienne did not fail to indicate on the title-pages of his works. It has been said since that Francis I. founded the Royal Printing House, but the truth is that Estienne kept these characters in his own office for use in the royal editions; they may now be seen in the Imprimerie Nationale at Paris.

Robert Estienne married the daughter of Josse Badius, of Asch—Badius Ascencianus, one of the first Parisian typographers of the time. We reproduce the mark of Badius, representing the interior of a printing house, and shall return in a special chapter to the functions of these workshops. Meantime it appears proper to present to the reader a printing office of the time of Robert Estienne and Geoffroy Tory.

Fig. 54.—Printing office of Josse Badius at the commencement of the sixteenth century.

Robert Estienne does not appear to have concerned himself much about the decoration of the Book. The purity of the text and the characters were essentials with him, erudition, and not art. He published many works in Latin and Greek, among them the *Thesaurus*, a great Latin dictionary published in 1532, also a Bible, with notes by Vatable, revised by Leon de Juda. From that came trouble. Leon de Juda was a partisan of Zwingli; the Sorbonne accused the Bible of leaning towards the Huguenots; Francis I. took the part of Estienne, but when that prince died Estienne fled to Geneva, where he was accused of having imported the royal types. The truth was that he simply imported the matrices.

Fig. 55.—Portrait of Nicholas Bourbon. Wood engraving of the commencement of the sixteenth century.

At this time everything served for the decoration of the Book: portraits, blazons, topographical plates, costumes, and emblems. Small portraits engraved on wood usually ornamented the works of the poets, like that of Nicholas Bourbon, for example, marvel of truth and skill. The blocks of frontispieces in the folios were multiplied; large initial letters, ingeniously engraved and stippled, like that at the commencement of this chapter, were used. Jacques Kerver reproduced in 1545 for himself, and with plates made for him, the famous *Songe de Poliphile*, published by Aldus in 1499. The widow of the publisher Denis Janot, Jeanne de Marnef, published one of the most delightful books of the time, *L'Amour de Cupidon et de Psyche* of Apuleius, with delicious figures in wood after Italian engravings. Many more could be named in the extraordinary profusion of charming books.

Fig. 56.—King and Death. Vignette from the "Dance of Death" by Holbein.

Without entering into detail, something must be said of Lyons, then a most extensive and prosperous centre of bookselling. Lyons had the signal honour of publishing first in France the celebrated cuts of the "Dance of Death" of Holbein, the Basle painter. Doubtless Treschel, the printer, was not the first, as a copy of a German edition is known, because in the Lyons edition the cuts are worn and broken. However, the Cabinet d'Estampes of Paris has some of the figures of the Dance with a German text, probably printed by Froben at Basle. Treschel's title was *Les Simulachres et Historiées Faces de la Mort autant elegamment pourtraictes que artificiellement imaginées*, and the volume in quarto was printed by Frelon. The *Icones veteris testamenti*, which preceded the publication of the "Dance of Death," had also been printed at Basle before Lyons.

With Holbein, as with Geoffroy Tory, we arrive at the zenith of illustration and marvellous skill of the engraver. If we were to institute comparisons, it was Hans Lutzelburger who cut the blocks after the designs of the Basle master, but, contrary to what generally happens, the translator reaches almost to the height of his model; the line is perfection itself, it is precise and intelligent, simple, and, above all, explicit. If the work of Lutzelburger be admitted, it must also be admitted that Holbein designed his cuts before 1526, date of the death of the Basle engraver; but it was precisely before 1526 that Holbein lived in Basle, and it was after he had travelled. We will add nothing to the universal praise of the book of Treschel, of Lyons; everything has been written of Holbein, and repetitions are unnecessary. We would ask the reader to compare the Francis I. of Tory and the King in Holbein's "Dance of Death;" there is a certain family resemblance between the two cuts, which is a singular honour for Tory.

At the commencement of the century Basle had a school of *Formschneiders* working for export. Besides the numerous products used at Lyons, it had also a trade in wood blocks, which, having been used, were afterwards sold. Among these exchanges of engravings were many plates of Brandt's "Ship of Fools," sold in 1520 to Galliot du Pré, publisher, of Paris, who used them in the *Eloge de la Folie* of Erasmus.

The reign of Francis I. saw a great advance in the national art of illustration. The arrival at the court of Italian artists of the decadence, such as Rosso and Primaticcio, produced a revolution in taste. The exaggerated slightness of the figures brought by these artists from beyond the Alps was considered as of supreme distinction; in their twisted draperies and mannered poses was seen a precious beauty that tempted the ready intelligence of the court of France. The simple and ingenuous figures of the old French artists were ranked among the refuse of another age, and their compositions were regarded with contempt, and deemed antique.

The rage for emblems and for allegories and mythological figures generally was well suited to these eccentric and bizarre inventions. From another side, an entire class of artists or artisans, book illustrators first, then enamellers and jewellers, made use of these Italian models, with which the King encumbered his galleries, and which, at great expense, covered the walls of Fontainebleau. One can understand what these skilful men made of such a movement and of so thoughtless an infatuation. The publishers saw the demand, and composed works of which the sale was assured by the subjects that they furnished to other designers. This explains the quantity of Alciati's "Emblems" and Ovid's "Metamorphoses" published at Lyons and Paris, and copied and recopied a hundred times by the art industries of the time. Without it the enormous success of mediocre productions, as the "Emblems," for example, in which the meaning of the enigma or rebus cannot always be seized, is ill understood. It was Alciati who made this literature the fashion. He was a sort of Epicurean and miserly jurisconsult, who had as many lords and masters on earth, as the kings and princes who liked to bid against each other to engage him. He had quitted Italy, seduced by the offers of Francis I., but when Sforza paid him a larger sum, he returned, giving as reason for his vacillation that the sun had to travel the earth and warm it by its rays; this was an emblematic answer, for his emblems had all the coarse, sceptical humour which not a few had then already discovered. At most these philosophical aphorisms, if we take them seriously, have their droll side in that their author often practised the reverse of his teaching. A miser, he abuses the avaricious; flying his country for the love of gain, he blames those to whom "a better condition is offered by strangers." Yet he is sometimes logical and consistent, as when he assures us that "poverty hinders the success of intelligence," and when, finally, lover of good cheer, he died of indigestion in 1550.

L'aage de Fer.

Fig. 57.—Page of the "Metamorphoses" of Ovid, by Petit Bernard. Edition of 1564.

His book of "Emblems" had a vogue that lasted until the seventeenth century, and repetitions were infinitely multiplied: at Paris by Wechel in 1534; at Lyons by Hans de Tornes, of Suabia, one of the greatest Lyons publishers; by Roville, also one of the first Lyons publishers, and by Bonhomme; at Venice by the Alduses; in fact, everywhere, translated into French, Spanish, and Italian.

Bernard Salomon, called *le Petit Bernard*, born at Lyons, was one of the designers of the school of Fontainebleau—that is to say, of the Franco-Italian school of which we have spoken above—who furnished many of the engravings for books printed at Lyons. He illustrated the edition of Alciati's "Emblems" published by Bonhomme in 1560; and designed skilful little plates, which, with the text, were surrounded by a border from the workshop of Geoffroy Tory, for Ovid's "Metamorphoses," published by Hans de Tornes in 1564. Bernard had all the defects and all the qualities of those of his time, from John Cousin to the least of them; he was a Primaticcio on a small scale, but agreeably so. His designs for the New Testament were also very careful, but in them more than elsewhere the manner and the affectation of the school of Fontainebleau are apparent.

Fig. 58.—Portraits of Madeleine, Queen of Scotland, and of Marguerite, Duchess of Savoy, after the originals of Cornelis of Lyons.

Fig. 59.—Portraits of Francis, dauphin, and of Charles, Duke of Angoûleme, after the originals of Cornelis of Lyons. Woodcuts taken from Roville's *Promptuaire des Médailles*.

The workshops of the second city of France, we see, had at this time attained considerable importance; but before the books of which we shall speak, Roville published two anonymous books, one *L'Entrée du Roi Henri II. à Lyon*, in 1549, ornamented with very graceful woodcuts, the other the *Promptuaire des Médailles*, comprising a series of charming portraits under the pretence of reproductions from the antique. The designs of the *Entrée* are often attributed to John Cousin, as it is a rule with certain amateurs to give a known name to a work; but it must be remembered that Lyons then had celebrated artists, Petit-Bernard, alluded to above, and Cornelis de la Haye, of whom we have more to say; and it is not necessary to go to Paris or to Rome to find the author of these illustrations.

Cornelis de la Haye was a painter who executed nearly the same work as Francis Clouet in Paris, portraits on panel, in a clear and harmonious tone, then much the fashion. During a journey of the King, he had, if Brantôme may be credited, portrayed the entire court, keeping the sketches for himself.

Ten or fifteen years after, Catherine de Medicis, passing through Lyons, saw these portraits and highly praised them, recognising the old costumes, astonished at the courtiers of the day, whom she had never seen in such dress. This artist is now known, thanks to various works that have been found, among others two portraits of the sons of Francis I., preserved by Gaignières, who attributed them resolutely to Cornelis, doubtless on the faith of inscriptions that have disappeared. Both of them were engraved on wood at Lyons and published in Roville's book the *Promptuaire des Médailles*, mentioned above, with small differences of detail altogether insignificant. It is not impossible then that Cornelis designed these portraits, and that they were drawn on wood after the cabinet models spoken of by Brantôme. The delicate figures of the *Promptuaire* are the work of a master; and the differences mentioned are those of the artist, not of the copyist, who would not be permitted to change anything. It is the first time, we believe, that these comparisons have been made; they will perhaps help the learned Lyonnais to pierce the mystery, but in any case our suppositions are more honourable to Cornelis de la Haye than the fancies of Robert Dumesnil (*Peintre-graveur Français*, tome vi., p. 343). To judge by the four little medallions here reproduced, the art of engraving on wood was rarely more skilful than in these portraits. It would not be astonishing if a man like Cornelis had designed the figures of the *Entrée de Henri II.* In any case, why should we choose John Cousin instead of Petit-Bernard? At this time, we know, the kings carried in their suite their ordinary painters; but we do not know that John Cousin followed the court to Lyons in 1549. He did not hold an official position, like Clouet.

Fig. 60.—Captain of foot from the *Entree de Henri II. à Lyon* (1549).

This artist produced well-authenticated works; one of them is signed, and leaves no doubt: the *Livre de Perspective de Jehan Cousin Senonois, Maistre Painctre*, published in 1560 by Jean le Royer, printer to the King for mathematics. This profession of printer for mathematics had its difficulties of engraving, for Le Royer tells us in his preface that he had himself finished the plates commenced by Albin Olivier. In another practical treatise, entitled *Livre de Portraiture*, published in 1593, John Cousin is styled *peintre géometrien*. It is beyond doubt that this master produced for many works figures and ornaments, but what were the books? The manner was then to repeat the engraved borders of titles, the *passe-partout*, in the centre of which the text was printed. Cousin designed many of these title-pages on wood; that of the *Livre de Portraiture* affords a curious element of comparison; but he was not by any means the inventor. In 1555 was sold at Antwerp a book printed from engraved plates after John Vriedman, by Gerard Juif, which is simply a collection of engravings for title-pages for the use of publishers.

Fig. 61.—Title of John Cousin's *Livre de Portraiture*, published in 1593 by Le Clerc. (The spot on the title is in the original, preserved among the prints of the Bibliothèque Nationale.)

It is about this time that metal plates may be seen in conjunction with wood engraving in the illustration of the Book, and the best artists attached their names to important publications of this kind. We have explained in a former chapter in what this process is least convenient in the impression of a book. In fact, two successive printings, that of the plates and that of the text, were additional trouble and a frequent cause of errors; but wood-cutting was somewhat abandoned in the middle of the sixteenth century, especially for separate plates, and engraved plates took a considerable importance under different artistic influences. The first was the facility of engraving a metal plate compared to the difficulty of cutting a wood block. It thus naturally happened that the artists of the burin wished to employ their art in illustration, and taste was soon drawn to the new process.

In France the first volume of this kind was printed in 1488 by Topie de Pymont in folio: the *Pérégrinations en Terre Sainte* of Bernard de Breydenbach, with figures on engraved plates copied from the Mayence edition of 1486. Since this manner was abandoned until about 1550, as much for the reasons given above as for others, we only meet with a stray plate now and again, which remains as a bait, and relates to nothing. Under the reign of Henri II. the smallness of the volumes did not always admit of wood engravings, and the artists in metal found a footing among illustrators; they made attempts, such as that of the *Histoire de Jason* of Réné Boivin in 1563, which came out under Charles IX. in a charming volume of engraved plates by P. Woériot.

The "Emblems" of Georgette de Montenay were also in the burlesque style of Alciati, but they had an advantage, as the author assures us:—

"Alciat fist des emblèmes exquis,
Lesquels, voyant de plusieurs requis,
Désir me prist de commencer les miens,
Lesquels je croy estre premiers chrestiens."

This orthodoxy does not make them more intelligible, but the engravings of Woériot, unskilful as they are, import an element of interest which surpasses the rest. It was always at Lyons, the rival and often the master of Paris in typography, that the author printed his work.

By the privilege dated 1566, five years before publication, we see that it is permitted to Peter Woériot, engraver of the Duke of Lorraine, to portray, engrave, and cut in copper the said figures called emblems for the time and term of five years (18th October, 1566). Peter Woériot sometimes signed his prints with the small Lorraine cross adopted by Geoffroy Tory's workshop, as may be seen in our engraving.

Copper plate engraving had by this time established itself, and the works that were so illustrated spread themselves. Du Cerceau published his admirable collection of *Plus Beaux Bastiments de France* in folio 1576-79, which had numerous plans and views of the royal and princely castles. Thevet put forth his *Cosmographie Universelle* and his *Hommes Illustres*, the latter adorned with skilfully engraved portraits. In Paris the publishers Mamert Patisson, who married the widow of Robert Estienne and took his mark, Adrien le Roy, and Robert Ballard, published the celebrated *Ballet Comique de la Royne Faict aux Nopces de Monsieur le Duc de Joyeuse*, composed by Balthasar de Beaujoyeux, valet de chambre to Henri III.; and in this book, in which were put hasty etchings, the King displayed all his immodesty and depravity. The Book has often had the unconscious mission of transmitting to posterity the unworthiness of its author or of its heroes. From this time the Book has left its golden age to enter into the boastings of courtiers and political abstractions.

Fig. 62.—Engraving by P. Woériot for Georgette de Montenay's *Emblèmes*.

Among the publications opposed to the Government of the time, the two associates James Tortorel and John Perrissin, of Lyons, had published a celebrated collection of plates on the religious wars that stained the reign of Charles IX. with blood. At first engraved on metal, these plates were worn out, and were gradually replaced by others engraved on wood, on which several artists worked, among them James le Challeux and also John de Gourmont, one of the most celebrated wood-cutters of the sixteenth century. This was a work composed of single leaves in folio size, which had an extraordinary sale among the religious people of the time.

At the same time, illustration on wood did not stand still. The portraits of authors diffused by the pencil of Clouet and his school were commonly put at the head of their works. We cannot say whether Clouet himself designed the portraits of Tiraqueau and of Taillemont in 1553; of Du Billon, the author of the *Fort Inexpugnable*, in 1555; Papon and Ambroise Paré in 1561; Grevin,

Ramus, and others; but the precision of these physiognomies recalls the peculiar manner of the French artists of the sixteenth century. The "Poems" of Ronsard in 1586 contains a series of very clever portraits, among them that of Muret, his commentator, one of the most perfect of its kind. Christopher de Savigny, author of the *Tableaux Accomplis de Tous les Arts Liberaux*, published by John and Francis de Gourmont in 1587, is represented at full length in the frontispiece of his work, offering the book to the Duc de Nevers, to whom it is dedicated. This plate in folio, probably engraved by John de Gourmont, is the best finished that we have seen. The work of Savigny, forgotten as it may be now, had a great reputation in its own time; and Bacon took from it the idea of his "Advancement of Learning."

Speaking of the Duc de Nevers, it will not be without interest to our readers to mention here a manuscript found by us in the Bibliothèque Nationale, which enables us to give an account of the work then necessary for the publication of an illustrated book. In 1577 the Duke arranged for the impression of an apologetic book, of which no trace remains; and his *intendant* writes a long letter to him on the subject of composition and bindings. It was necessary that the work should be produced quickly, bound and gilt, for presents. The *intendant* thinks calf will be the most expeditious covering. "It would be much the best to use black or red calf, ... well gilt above, and not vellum, which is a thin parchment that quickly shrinks." The statements of this man of business show that five proofs of each sheet were taken for typographical correction, and that twelve full days were wanted for the binding. The most interesting part of this memoir is that which treats of the engraving on wood of the portrait. The plate was designed by an artist who had afterwards gone away; it was not satisfactory, but the ornaments would pass. The *intendant* proposes to "fix a little piece of wood in the block that could be drawn upon." Here we see correction by elimination. The pear-wood on which the original figure was engraved was to be cut out, and a square of boxwood substituted, "forasmuch as in this task the pear-wood, which is the successful, well-cut block, is the wood that is harder."

Fig. 63.—Portrait of Christopher Plantin, printer of Antwerp. Engraved by Wierix.

The portrait of the Duchesse de Nevers was better, yet the pear-wood had given way under the work. "That of Madame is more passable. Nevertheless, there is still something to say to one eye. The wood cannot carry the subtlety of the line." Here, in a few clear and explicit lines by a man of the time, we see the economy of a publication of the sixteenth century, at a time when wood engraving was declining, to give place to engraving on metal, which was soon to reign supreme, through the most important book house of the century: the Plantins of Antwerp.

Christopher Plantin, like Jenson, came originally from Tours. After having learned his art with Macé at Caen, he went to Paris, from which the wars soon drove him. He left for the Low Countries, and there Philip II. nominated him as chief printer—"architypographus." Established at Antwerp in 1555, he surrounded himself, as had the Estiennes and Alduses, with most of the learned and literary men of his time, among them Justus Lipsius, to whom Balzac attributed the Latin prefaces signed by Plantin. It is certain that he was neither an Estienne nor an Aldus. His artistic probity caused him to submit the proofs of his works to strangers, with promise of recompense for faults indicated; the Estiennes employed the same system. Plantin, not to be behind any of his contemporaries in typographical perfection, brought from France the celebrated type-founder William Lebé, and charged him to furnish a special fount.[5] Under the orders of Philip II., he printed the celebrated Polyglot Bible, in eight folio volumes, absolutely perfect in its execution; unfortunately the Spanish Government, having advanced funds in the course of publication, prosecuted him with the utmost rigour to obtain repayment. This very nearly shut up his printing house, but he took courage and overcame his difficulties, until he became, in 1589, the year of his death, the principal publisher of Flanders. His mark was a hand holding a compass, with the motto "Labore et constantia."

[5] In the Bibliothèque Nationale is a copy of an octavo *Album de Caractères*, in which Lebé has written, "This gloss, made in Paris (1574) by me, is my fourteenth letter, and the text is made on the pattern of the preceding one for size, but of a better art; and from this was printed the great Bible of Antwerp by Plantin, to whom I sold a fount" (folio 6). On folio 20 he wrote, "I do not know whence came this small Hebrew that I received from Plantin to make a smaller one for him. He sent me this half-sheet, and I have not seen at Venice another part."

Fig. 64.—Plantin's mark.

Plantin died at the age of seventy-four, leaving a prosperous business to be divided between his three daughters. His first house at Antwerp employed seventeen presses even at the time when he was in trouble, and he had branches at Paris and Leyden, of less consequence. His second daughter married Moretus, and to him descended the Antwerp workshop; he and his descendants continued the printing house until recently; the house of the great printer and publisher is now a typographical museum. The Plantin printing office—"Officina Plantiniana"—was as well managed by its descendants as by himself. The fashion of engraving in metal spread itself before the death of the head of the house, and his successors continued it. The principal engravers with the burin of the Low Countries were employed by them: Wierix, Galle, Pass, Mallery, Van Sichern; it was a real school of illustration, that created by degrees a precious and sustained style, not without influence on the artists of that epoch. It was from this particular manner that came Thomas de Leu and Leonard Gaultier in France; and from Antwerp came those small religious figures that have lasted to our time in their incomprehensible mysticism.

The title-pages of the Plantin printing office inaugurated the *passe-partout* engraved by the burin, overloaded and complicated, of which the seventeenth century took advantage. To tell the truth, these elaborate displays, blackened by ink, do not accord well with the titles; and there is a long distance between this decadence and the books ornamented with wood blocks by the Italians and French of the commencement of the century. Exception must be made in favour of Rubens, who designed many of these titles. The heavy and squat architecture of the time was least of all appropriate to these decorations, which wanted grace. It passed from Plantin into France through the engravers; it went to Rome with Martin de Vos and John Sadeler; it imposed itself everywhere; and from that day to this it has not ceased. At the time of which we write it had taken its flight in France, and spread itself in Europe with extraordinary success. Engraving in relief, holding its own until then, gave way little by little before this invasion. When Henri IV. mounted the throne wood engraving had finished its upward movement, it still remained in the *canards*, or popular pieces sold at low prices, but it is easy to see what these hasty vignettes are worth.

ICONES VETERVM
ALIQVOT, AC RECEN
TIVM MEDICORVM
PHILOSOPHORVMQVE
ELOGIOLIS SVIS
EDITÆ, OPERA
L. SAMBVCI

Fig. 65.—Frontispiece of a book from Plantin's printing office. Metal engraving.

We have now seen the history of the Book and its decoration in the sixteenth century in France: at first French epics in Italy, books of hours, romances of chivalry; then about 1550, with the reign of Henri II., the religious pamphlets commenced, bookselling spread itself; the strife between illustrations on metal plates and those in relief assumed shape, it continued under Henri III., and terminated abruptly by the victory of the first at the extreme end of the century. With political passions, printing had become a weapon of warfare, which it will never cease to be. They knew in the sixteenth century what perfidious accusations or excessive praises were worth. The Book followed the fate of its author. If the writer was burned, so was his book. Witness the *Christianismi Restitutio* of the Catholic Servetus, printed at Vienne, in Dauphiné, and consigned to the flames with its author at Geneva in 1553. A single copy was saved from the fire, and is now preserved in the Bibliothèque Nationale; it is the identical copy annotated by Colladon, the accuser of the unhappy Servetus, and still bears traces of fire on its leaves.

Typography and the illustration of the Book in England in the sixteenth century did not make the same progress as in France and Italy. Much good work was done, but it was mostly with foreign material. Type was obtained from French and Dutch founders, and most of the woodcuts had the same origin. In the early part of the century most of the publications were translations of popular foreign books, such as Voragine's "Golden Legend," Caxton's translations of Cicero, Boetius, etc. Too many restrictions and privileges obtained to encourage or allow of the establishment of an English school, which was to come later with the spread of wealth and education. Books were mostly printed in Gothic type, or "black letter," and the woodcuts were of the coarsest kind. An exception was the beautiful Prayer-book of John Day, 1578, known as Queen Elizabeth's Prayer-book, from the fine portrait of the Queen, which we reproduce, on the previous page; but in this the woodcuts were designed by Albert Dürer and Hans Holbein. Pynson was the first to use Roman type in England, in the *Oratio in pace nuperrimâ*, 1518, quarto; and the first English Bible in Roman type was printed at Edinburgh in 1576. It is thought that until about 1600 printers were their own type-founders, as no record exists of founding as a separate trade until that time.

Fig. 66.—Portrait of Queen Elizabeth from the "Book of Christian Praiers," printed by John Day, 1578.

The greatest achievement of the sixteenth century in England was the printing of the first English Bible, in Coverdale's translation, in 1535, folio, but even this was printed abroad, the latest investigation giving it to Van Meteren at Antwerp. The woodcuts in it are by Hans Sebald Beham; we reproduce one representing Cain killing Abel. Tyndall had previously printed abroad an English New Testament. Another importation was Brandt's "Shyp of Folys," printed by Pynson, 1509, and John Cawood, 1570, the woodcuts in both being copied from the originals before referred to.

Fig. 67.—Woodcut from Coverdale's Bible, 1535. Cain killing Abel.

Folio was the size usually adopted, and in this size the series of chronicles appeared: Arnold, printed abroad in 1502; Fabian, in 1516; Froissart, by Pynson, in two volumes, 1523-5; Harding, by Grafton, 1543; Hall, by the same, 1548; Holinshed, in two volumes, 1577. In the same size Chaucer was first given to the world entire by T. Godfrey in 1532, and many times reprinted, and Sir Thomas More in 1557. Polemical and religious treatises were mostly printed in quarto, as were the poets: Spenser's *Faerie Queene*, in 1590; Langland's *Pierce Plowman*, in 1550; and Sidney's *Arcadia*, in 1590. Plays were also printed in quarto, in which shape at the end of the century some of Shakespeare's single plays were issued.

From the great perfection to which the liturgies, or books of hours, had been brought by Vostre, Verard, and others in France, it is not perhaps extraordinary that the service books for English use should have been mostly printed abroad. Those for Salisbury and York were produced at Paris, Rouen, and Antwerp. A Salisbury Primer in English was printed by John Kyngston and Henry Sutton in 1557, and Wynken de Worde printed a York Manual in 1509. The first English Common Prayer Book, known as Edward VI.'s, was printed by Grafton in 1549, who also printed in 1545 Henry VIII.'s Primer in Latin and English. Edward's book is curious as having on the last page a royal order as to the price at which it was to be sold: "No maner of persone shall sell the present Booke vnbounde aboue the price of two shillynges and two pence. And bound in Forell for ii*s*. x*d*., and not aboue. And the same bound in Shepes Lether for iii*s*. iii*d*., and not aboue. And the same bounde in paste or in boordes, in Calues Lether, not aboue the price of iiii*s*. the pece."Cranmer's Catechism was printed by Nicholas Hill in 1548, with twenty-nine woodcuts by Hans Holbein, one of which we reproduce, representing Christ casting out devils.

Translations from the classics were popular, and in the second half of the century arose that passion for voyage and travel which has so largely contributed to the wealth and extension of England. This was begun by Eden's translation of Peter Martyr's "Decades of the New World; or, West India," London, 1555, quarto, followed by Hakluyt's "Principall Navigations, Voyages, and Discoveries," 1589, folio. Many accounts of single voyages and discoveries were issued, and the taste thus created culminated in the establishment of the East India Company in the last year of thecentury.

The first specimen of copper plate engraving for books in England is a frontispiece to Galen's *De Temperamentis*, printed at Cambridge 1521, and the number of books containing copper plates engraved before 1600 is extremely limited, the most notable being portraits of Queen Elizabeth, Lord Leicester, and Lord Burleigh in Archbishop Parker's Bible of 1568; Saxton's Atlas, 1579, the first atlas in England; Harrington's translation of Ariosto, 1591, with forty-seven engraved plates.

Fig. 68.—Woodcut by Hans Holbein from Cranmer's Catechism, 1548.

The first printer at Cambridge was John Siberch, 1521. Peter of Treves established himself at Southwark in 1514. Among his productions is a Higden's *Polychronicon*, 1527, folio. John Oswen printed at Ipswich 1538, and among the English towns in which printers established themselves in the century were York, Canterbury, Tavistock, Norwich, and Worcester.

The establishment of the Reformed Church, and the diffusion of education among the people which followed, created an original English school of literature in the sixteenth century, and this gave employment and great impetus to typography in England, so that by the time we reach the end of the century we find a great improvement in the art of the Book, to be carried to still greater perfection in the next.

CHAPTER IV.

1600 TO 1700.

Tendencies of the regency of Marie de Medicis—Thomas de Leu and Leonard Gaultier—J. Picart and Claude Mellan—Lyons and J. de Fornazeris—The Book at the beginning of the seventeenth century in Germany, Italy, and Holland—Crispin Pass in France—The Elzevirs and their work in Holland—Sebastian Cramoisy and the Imprimerie Royale—Illustration with Callot, Della Bella, and Abraham Bosse—The publishers and the Hotel de Rambouillet—The reign of Louis XIV., Antoine Vitré syndic at his accession—His works and mortifications; the polyglot Bible of Le Jay—Art and illustrators of the grand century—Sébastien Leclerc, Lepautre, and Chauveau—Leclerc preparing the illustration and decoration of the Book for the eighteenth century—The Book in England in the seventeenth century.

Fig. 69.—Letter engraved by A. Bosse.

NOW we have arrived at a critical epoch, in which the science of the old printers transformed itself gradually into commerce, in which taste lost itself under the influence of religious architecture. The title of the Book represents the portico of a cathedral, with columns, mitred saints, and crosses, of little decorative aspect. Figures on copper plates replaced the foliage and arabesques of the older booksellers. Through the Plantins and their imitators, the architectural passion was far spread. It inundated France, ran through Germany and Italy, and reigned pre-eminent in Holland. Literary taste also underwent change; manners were no longer those of the sixteenth century: bold, free, and gay; from the religious wars a certain hypocrisy arose; bombast replaced the natural; the gods were preparing, as a contemporary said, to receive Louis and his spirit.

It is not that artists were wanting at the opening of the seventeenth century who could, in giving scope to their talent, show themselves worthy successors of those who went before them. Unhappily the booksellers no longer had a loose rein; they had the rope, for they were hung or burned at the least infraction of political or religious propriety. Yet the reign of Henri IV. was relatively an easier period for the artisans of the Book, in which they were less confined to the strict terms of excessive regulations; but after this prince severity increased, and during the year 1626 a new law was promulgated punishing with death the printers or distributers of prohibited books. Doubtless the books that were thus secretly sold, and prohibited in defence of good manners, were neither *chefs-d'œuvre* of typography nor art. The author threw off the indecencies by which he hoped to make profit and fame, regardless of type or illustration. But during the regency of Marie de Medicis, it was not only the authors of a bad standard that were in danger of being hung; the printer or seller of the pamphlet or book of a reputed heterodox author was also hung, and it became difficult to steer safely among the prohibitions. Enormous numbers of works were made with frontispieces decorated with colonnades and mitred saints, and bearing high-sounding titles of sound orthodoxy. A somewhat gross mysticism, from the office of Plantin, formed the most solid stock of every respectable dealer.

Fig. 70.—Title of the *Metanealogie*, engraved by Leonard Gaultier.

Under Henri IV. and the minority of Louis XIII., two French illustrators received from the school of Antwerp their inspiration for the ornament of the Book. Thomas de Leu, probably from Flanders, was allied with the old Parisian painter and engraver of celebrated portraits, Antoine Caron, in furnishing the engraved plates for the *Images de Plate Peinture des Deux Philostrates, Sophistes Grecs*, Paris, Claude Cramoisy, 1609, folio; and Leonard Gaultier, his contemporary, collaborated with Jaspar Isaac and other artists in the Book. Leonard Gaultier contributed most to spread in France the Plantinian style, and his somewhat cold but characteristic talent suited this art more than that of any one else then could. He was an engraver of portraits, now rare and valuable, in the style of Wierix or Thomas de Leu; but, at the demand of publishers and booksellers, he composed other plates, at first historical figures representing the royal family and the nobles for the publisher Leclerc, in a simple and true manner; he also designed pious figures, recording a miracle or representing the ceremonies of a jubilee and other devotional things. But he made his great success in the composition of frontispieces to theological and pious works, printed for nearly all the booksellers. Leonard Gaultier had a fashion of his own with pilasters and Grecian columns, under which he boldly placed entire councils of cardinals and bishops; witness the heading of the *Bibliotheca Veterum Patrum*, into which he crowded nearly forty figures. He united also with a certain grace the sacred and the profane, placing among ideal saints the sinning fine ladies of the time, with their large collarettes and jewels falling on naked breasts. The work of Andrew Valladier, chaplain of the King, entitled *Métanéalogie Sacrée*, published by Peter Chevallier in 1609, was adorned with a title of this particular kind, in which Gaultier had no rival, and which preserves the precision of Flemish masters in the detail of ornaments of the toilet.

He was one of the first to work for Sebastian Cramoisy, printer and publisher, who had established his shop in the Rue St. Jacques at the sign of the "Stork." We shall have occasion to speak of him later in connection with the Royal Printing House, of which he was the first director; he is mentioned now because in 1611 Leonard Gaultier engraved for him the frontispiece of *L'Aigle Français*, a collection of sermons by Thomas Girault. The publisher used the same plate in 1618 for the sermons of Raymond de Hézèque.

Besides the publications of Sebastian Cramoisy and Chevallier, Leonard Gaultier adorned also those of Nicholas Buon and many other publishers of the time in Paris and Lyons. With such a profusion of works emanating from a single artist, without reckoning those which were produced in great quantity by men of less note, wood engraving was dead. At most it dared to put a wood block of a printer's mark on a title; more ordinarily this mark was not alone sufficient, and showed the disdain in which taste then held woodcutting. Thus goes fashion, heedless of the most elementary rules of art. To put type within an engraved title, or to ornament a printed text with engravings, is a heresy of principle that was established in the eighteenth century, by the strength of its cleverness and talent. But at the beginning of the seventeenth, in spite of Leonard Gaultier or Thomas de Leu, these overloaded titles, overpowering the opening of the Book, offend the eye by their excessive blackness, and incontestably make us regret the admirable frontispiece on wood of the preceding century.

This is all the ornament, properly so called, of the reign of Louis XIII. Leonard Gaultier composed also small vignettes for an edition of Homer, but they are mediocre and unskilful, and it must be said that there were others following the same path. John Picart made a frontispiece with architecture and figures for the *Histoire de la Maison de Châtillon-sur-Marne* for account of Sebastian Cramoisy. A cold and hard artist he was, the rival of Gaultier, and one of the most employed of the vignette engravers of Paris. There was also Jaspar Isaac, a mediocre craftsman, but who could design clever titles, among them that of the continuation of the *Annales* of Baronius for the publisher Denis de la Noue. Then Claude Mellan, whose great and clever talent did not disdain second-rate works, in which he gave free play to his burin. It must be said, however, that his bold touch did not well accommodate itself to reduced spaces, and that he was not working in the field necessary to his inventive powers. We mention his portrait of Louis XIV. at the head of the *Code Louis XIV.*; the title of the *Perfection du Chrestien*, in which is included a portrait of Cardinal Richelieu, A. Vitré, 1647, folio; that of the *Instruction du Dauphin* for Cramoisy, 1640; that of the works of St. Bernard for the Royal Printing House; and, perhaps the best of all, the *Poésies* of Pope Urban VIII., of which we here give a copy.

Fig. 71.—Title engraved by Claude Mellan for Urban VIII.'s *Poésies*, printed at the Royal Printing House, in 1642.

Lyons did not remain far behind in the movement, but how changed from its great reputation of the sixteenth century! J. de Fornazeris engraved the frontispieces to Justus Lipsius, published by Horace Cardon in 1613. Peter Favre and Audran imitated them. C. Audran designed for Claude Landry the *Theologia Naturalis* of Theophilus Reynaud, and the bookseller Picquet ordered from him the title for the *Annales Minorum* in 1628. Everywhere taste was modelled on the works of the capital, to name only the principal centres, Rouen, Rheims, Sens, down to Venes, a small town of Tarn, where William de Nautonnier published in 1603 his curious book *Mécométrie*, whose frontispiece was bordered by views of cities, with an equestrian portrait of

King Henry.

And if we pass to Germany, we find Mayence with mediocre engravings for titles according to the formula and process used elsewhere, the title of the *Droit Civil* of Aymar Vailius, that of the works of St. Bonaventura in 1609 for the bookseller Antoine Hiérat, and that of the *Viridarium Virtutûm*, rather cleverly treated by the burin in 1610. What a period had passed since Gutenberg, Fust, and Schoeffer! There was still one Yves Schoeffer at Mayence, but only the name lived; nothing more remained of the old printers of the other century. It was the same at Bamberg, Cologne, Nuremberg, and Basle, in all the cities that made the honour of typography and the Book in former times. Cologne was neither better nor worse favoured than others. The booksellers Boetzer, Kinck, and De Binghy had passable engravings for their titles; and the Commentaries of Salmeron may be mentioned, with portraits from the German originals of the fifteenth century. At Nuremberg there was a curious specimen treating of natural history by Basil Besler, in which the artist gives the interior of a zoological cabinet of the time; but the blocks and the typography of the city of Koburger are wanting. Basle held its own later in relief engraving. Meantime there was a mediocre set of the Dance of Death on copper, published by Miegen, 1621.

At Jena and Frankfort-on-the-Main were prosperous printing houses, but engravings and ornamentation were neglected. Frankfort employed the frontispiece in the *Traité du Commerce* of Sigismond Scaccia, published by Zuner in 1648; it was divided into compartments, in which the Bourse, the Exchange, and the port of the city were represented.

It is scarcely necessary to mention the Italian cities which followed the movement. Venice from the middle of the sixteenth century had used engraved frontispieces, among which was that of Domenic Zenoi for the *Portraits des Hommes Illustres* of Nicholas Valegio. In the same city James Piccini worked for account of Sgava in 1648, but he was equally at the service of Roman publishers, for whom he designed a number of titles. Along with him Frederic Greuter adorned the publications of Alexander Zanetti, not without talent, but without individuality. Bologna, Brescia, Florence, and Naples, had no original sentiment; they followed indifferently the manner of the day.

In Holland, artists were rather numerous. The family of the Passes designed vignettes for books, and engraved frontispieces, admirably studied and composed. The clear and truly personal style of their works places their illustrations in the first rank among those of their time. They had, at the same time, the genius that created and the intelligent burin that faithfully translated an idea. They imagined with art the scenes that they depicted without at all copying their predecessors. From 1599, the date of the publication of the *Hortus Deliciarum*, one of their best works, up to about 1623, they were in Holland, at Arnheim and at Amsterdam. In 1623 we find one of them, the most celebrated, Crispin the younger, designing figures for the *Manège Royal* of Pluvinel, published by Angelier in Paris, and for another edition, with folding plates, in 1624 for William Lenoir, at the sign of the "White Rose Crowned." This magnificent work, in which the King, Louis XIII., is represented receiving lessons from the rider Pluvinel, had a third and more complete reimpression in 1625 with another publisher, Michael Nivelle. Here we see the Dutch accredited in France, in Paris, in the city then the most ready to understand and pay for the works of eminent artists. In 1624 Gombauld published an *Endymion*—Boileau later associated Gombauld with other poets to declare him a maker of pitiable sonnets—Nicholas Buon, the bookseller named above, undertook the publication, and employed Pass, Leonard Gaultier, and J. Picart to furnish plates in octavo size. Heavy and black as were these vignettes, they do not the less make a good appearance in the edition of the forgotten poet; and it is due to truth to recognise how much Pass was above his collaborators. The following year, 1625, he engraved the *Dionysiaques* of Nonus, for Robert Fouet, and the *Roman des Romans* of Du Verdier, comprising more than ten engravings, in a very free and bold manner. The *Berger Extravagant* and the *Académie de l'Espée* came in 1628, among numerous others.

Fig. 72.—Title of Pluvinel's *Manège Royal*, engraved by Crispin Pass in 1624.

To speak truly, Crispin Pass did not devote himself entirely to Parisian publishers; he always preserved interests in Flanders so as to return there from time to time; but he did not find in his own country the ready and assured sales of Paris. Still the city of Leyden had then one of the most renowned workshops of typography; the Elzevirs had commenced to make a good place for themselves among the printers of Europe by the extreme correctness of their editions, the distinctness of their work, and their marvellous art in the taste and economy of the Book. In reality, the sizes and characters of their books were very small, but if the smallness of the page did not allow room for vignette or ornament, they bore a certain practical elegance that was not without charm. The origin of the printing house was due to Louis Elzevir, who published in 1592 an edition of Eutropius at Leyden. He left sons, who associated themselves together, and founded a house which was unrivalled.

Fig. 73.—Title of the *Imitation* of the Elzevirs.

Bonaventure Elzevir, grandson of Louis, was the most illustrious of this family, so remarkably devoted to its art. He took Abraham as partner, and together they put forth those little Latin classics in duodecimo of which the value is now so great. Among others, Pliny issued from their presses in the year 1635, in three volumes, Virgil in 1636, and Cicero in 1642. To-day amateurs, above all those afflicted with bibliomania, hunt for unbound Elzevirs, because they have full margins. From about 1633 to 1639 these volumes were composed of paper of rather small size, making a page of a hundred and thirty to a hundred and thirty-three millimetres; from 1639 onwards the paper was larger, and the page from about a hundred and thirty-five to a hundred and thirty-seven. One must be a book-lover to understand the interest attaching to these figures, and employ his entire activity in the discovery of these undiscoverable books, which are concealed as soon as they are met with.

One of the most esteemed of their works is the *De Imitatione* of Thomas à Kempis, printed by John and Daniel Elzevir about 1653, and known as the edition without date. But as the association of John and Daniel is known to have lasted from 1652 to 1654, the date 1653 appears to be very plausible. We reproduce the entire title of this typographical *bijou*, which merited a cleverer engraver.

The rarest of all the numerous Elzevirs, possibly by reason of the popularity of its subject, is the *Pastissier François*, Louis and Daniel Elzevir, Amsterdam, 1655, of which M. Morgand had an uncut copy, measuring a hundred and forty-three millimetres, in 1878. The Benzon copy sold in 1875 for three thousand two hundred and fifty-five francs.

It is to be remarked that the Elzevirs frequently avoided dating or even signing their books, for reasons easy to comprehend. Publishing numerous works, they were afraid of compromising themselves in the eyes of the powerful, and they let them go forth without any trade mark. These artists in typography were, besides, the most prudent and subtle of men. Working at a time when bookselling had become an acknowledged commerce, and a trade requiring all the skill and resources of others, they wisely availed themselves of these, gathering for themselves honour and profit without having done more than seize their opportunity. Employing the characters of Claude Garamond, of James Sanlecques, and the papers of Angoulême, M. Didot thence claims them as French publishers.

In France the Elzevirs had no rivals; but a fashion was introduced from the end of the sixteenth century of associating together publishers in the production of important and costly books. There were, among others, the company of the "Grand Navire" in 1610, of the "Source" in 1622, and of the "Soleil" in 1629. In 1631 several publishers united and founded a second company of the "Grand Navire." These were the two Cramoisys, Sebastian and Gabriel, Denis Béchet, John Branchu, Denis Moreau, Claude Sonnius, and Denis Thierry. The associates took a ship as their mark, but without putting their names on the masts, as the original company of the "Grand Navire" had done. They published, at common expense and divided profits, great works, of which each one of them had the right of sale, but of course reserving to themselves the right to publish such others as they pleased. Sebastian Cramoisy passes as the chief, the moral director of another company, formed to publish the Fathers of the Church, with the royal types, a company affiliated to the "Grand Navire" and signed in 1638 by Denis Moreau, Gille Morel, Stephen Richer, Claude Sonnius, and Gabriel Cramoisy. But as regards their personal works, if they had neither the perfection nor the aspect of those of Froben, Aldus, the Estiennes, or even of Plantin, they at least surpassed the French books of the time. Formerly syndic of the Corporation in 1602, twenty-nine years before the constitution of the "Grand Navire," Cramoisy was besides sheriff of Paris, and he exercised his trade in a shop in the Rue St. Jacques which had been that of Father Nivelle, the *doyen* of booksellers, who died in 1603 at the age of eighty years.

The position of Cramoisy made it natural for Cardinal de Richelieu to fix his eyes on him for the direction of the Royal Printing House. This establishment, founded by the King in 1640, was installed within the Louvre, in a long series of rooms which formed a workshop without rival in the world. Sublet des Noyers was named superintendent, Trichet du Fresne corrector; and under this triple direction the presses commenced to work. The first book was the *Imitation de Jésus-Christ*, dated 1640, folio, a fine book enough, but not to be compared to the Elzevir editions. The types used in this book are attributed to Claude Garamond, founder of the sixteenth century, to whom are due the Greek types of Francis I. With the Royal Printing House, as often happens with State enterprises, the cost was great, and the return nothing. Only a few years after its foundation it had swallowed up nearly 400,000 livres, a very heavy sum for a badly balanced treasury; it had produced sixty or seventy volumes of moderate value; and after Cramoisy the management was so little in earnest that it turned the workshops into a stable, called "the little stable of the King," at the commencement of the eighteenth century.

Fig. 74.—Plate taken from the *Lumière du Cloistre*. Copper plate by Callot.

To return to the artists of the Book under Louis XIII. and Cardinal Richelieu, we must go back a little, before the foundation of the Royal Printing House, and we shall find the French school of illustration at a time when Callot was giving it a vigorous lift and trying to do away with its affected and hard style. It must be acknowledged that Callot was not a vignettist, a special designer; his art aimed higher, and ordinarily succeeded better; yet he did not disdain frontispieces, and made them for the *Coustumier de Lorraine*, the *Harpalice* of Bracciolini, and for a crowd of others of which the enumeration would be tedious. Certain of his works passed into Italy, where they raised a little the debased level of the Book. Then he adorned several works with etchings, among them the *Lumière du Cloistre*, published by Francis Langlois 1646. It was one of the symbolic and sententious works with which the public taste is never satiated, and a kind of guide for the priest. At the bottom of the little etching here given, representing birds falling from a tree, we read,—

"Ses petits hors du nid le courbeau jette en bas,
Lorsque par leur blancheur ils lui sont dissemblables.
Le bon prélat de mesme au cloistre n'admet pas
Ceux qui n'ont rien d'esgal à ses mœurs vénérables."

Callot also made another set of emblems on the life of the Virgin Mary, and published in 1620 a series of prints in quarto for the tragedy of *Soliman* of Bonarelli, for the account of Cecconnelli. France imposed herself on fallen Italy, she got her works dispersed there, and if an engraver arose there, he did not disdain to consecrate himself to France. Witness Della Bella, who went from Italy to France, where he was taken under the protection of Cardinal Richelieu. It was about the time of the establishment of the Royal Printing House, and it was expected that employment would be found at once for him.

Callot was the model chosen by the young Italian artist, and this choice might have been less happy. Della Bella took from his master the philosophic vein, the drollery of design, which he exercised at first in humorous frontispieces, among others that of Scarron's works, where nine fish-women, taking the place of the Muses, dance around the poet. But he passed from gay and pleasant to severe, and made large pages of architecture for serious titles. In 1649 he designed the plates for the large and undigested volume of Valdor on Louis XIII., published by Antoine Estienne at the Royal Printing House. His success was not there; Della Bella was a painter of groups, of ornaments, of subjects somewhat heavy and overdrawn, but which, after numerous transformations, opened a new way to the vignettists of the eighteenth century.

Fig. 75.—Title of the *Manière Universelle*, by Desargues, in 1643, by Abraham Bosse.

With Abraham Bosse the decoration of the Book took a considerable extension. Numerous and charming ornamented letters, heads of pages, and tailpieces appear. There are few artists that have done so much as he for graceful illustration and harmony between the vignette and the printed page. His prodigious fecundity made him attempt every style; and after the gaieties of the print in which he laughed with his contemporaries, he adopted a grave air to trace more severe subjects on copper. However, the book entitled *La Manière Universelle*, by Desargues, with numerous geometrical figures and an agreeable frontispiece, bearing the dedication to the Seigneur de Noyers, superintendent of the Royal Printing House, was a critical work, in which Bosse, under a serious standard, did not spare an enemy. We do not bear ill-will to the artist, however, for the following year he published fourteen plates for the Suetonius printed at the Louvre.

He successively designed plates for the *Histoire de St. Louis*, numerous vignettes for pious books, figures for the *Pucelle* of Chapelain and for the *Larcins de la Fortune*. He was always himself, refined and ingenious, whether in the most barren or the most complicated subjects.

Fig. 76.—Print by Abraham Bosse representing the booksellers of the Palace under Louis XIII.

He has left us in a celebrated print a representation of a bookseller's shop of his time. It is for us an interesting page, in which is shown simply and rather naïvely the picturesque side of these stores, with the dealer and his wife selling new works to their customers. The shop is compact, and very much like the open-air stalls of to-day; posting-bills above the shelves indicate the "new books;" and if the inscriptions given by Bosse be credited, the Palace dealer offered his books with singular eclecticism: Boccaccio, Aretin, the *Astrée* of D'Urfé, the Bible, and Machiavelli. In the hands of the woman is seen the romance *Marianne*:

"Icy les cavaliers les plus adventureux
En lisant les romans s'animent à combattre;
Et de leur passion les amants langoureux
Flattent les mouvements par des vers de théâtre,"

says the text of Bosse. What was commonly done then is still done, shopping and rummaging the stalls, and those of the Palace were attractive.

If we credit Sauval, the great number of booksellers, in the middle of the century, was due to the wits of the Hotel de Rambouillet. The passion for novelty, for recent works, had produced that quantity of publishers, he says, that we have seen on the Pont Neuf, and that we still see to-day at the Palace and the University, but of which the number is so multiplied in all these places that in the Palace they count more than other dealers; and as to the neighbourhood of the University, they are obliged, in order to lodge the rest, to extend the ancient bounds from St. Yves to the river (Sauval, *Antiquités de Paris*, viii., 354).

In fact, each year saw an increase in the number of publishers in corporation, with syndicate and adjuncts. Under the reign of Louis XIII., the single year 1610 had fifty to take rank, and among them Antoine Vitré, who was to become the most illustrious of his contemporaries. But, as there were no more than six printers, it may be inferred that all the rest were booksellers, in the true sense of the word, of those who encumbered afterwards the great *salle* of which Sauval speaks. Antoine Vitré was syndic in May, 1643, on the accession of Louis XIV. He had four adjuncts. With him the Book marked the solemn style that the commencement of the century had given to it. Royal printer for the Oriental languages from 1621, he undertook a Syriac work, the first that was attempted in Paris. The project of a Polyglot Bible gave him the idea of acquiring for the King the Oriental manuscripts and matrices of Savary de Brèves. The King left to him the care of negotiating the business, but did not reimburse him without numerous difficulties, in the midst of which the printer was made to lose the means of conveniently continuing his trade. The advocate Le Jay charging himself with the enormous expenses necessitated by the Polyglot Bible, it was composed in the hope that Cardinal Richelieu would pay the cost. He was willing to do so, but required that his name should figure on the book; and as Le Jay, an independent man, formally opposed it, Vitré met with ill-will from the Minister, which increased from day to day. In 1645 the impression was finished, but Le Jay was ruined, and if we admire the paper, the type, and the extraordinary size of the nine volumes of the Polyglot Bible, we find in it so many faults, errors, and misprints that it has fallen to nearly nothing, hardly being worth its binding. There were terrible mortifications in the business, and Vitré had to submit to them more than any one. Nevertheless he did not let his presses stand still, and he published successively Arabic, Turkish, and Persian works. His action against the Savary heirs, as representing the King, in the acquisition mentioned above, continued also after the impression of the Bible, and hindered his progress. He struggled on; and the assembly of clergy, of which he was the printer, sought to help him out of his difficulties. The matter being once terminated, the Cardinal being dead, and Vitré having been named by Colbert director of the Royal Printing House in place of Cramoisy, he died in his turn, and was later accused of having destroyed the types and matrices of the Polyglot Bible, so that they should not be used after him. This fable, long accredited, has since been ascertained to be false, for the punches and matrices passed to the Royal Library, thence to the Royal Printing House, reorganised in 1691.

Antoine Vitré, in spite of his misfortunes, was a great personage. He was painted by Champagne and engraved by Morin, as was Richelieu himself. The portrait was reproduced in the book of M. Delaborde, *La Gravure* (p. 189). Such was the man whom we meet at the beginning of the reign of Louis XIV. as syndic of booksellers; and it was by no means a sinecure, a canonry giving honour and profit, quite the other way. With the Draconian rules on the subject, the syndic assumed a heavy burden towards the King, as well as towards his kinsmen. Religious quarrels envenomed questions, and the revocation of the Edict of Nantes was to have for its immediate corollary new and more severe royal ordinances.

The reign of Louis XIV. saw the zenith of engraving with the burin, but not that of printing or illustration. Doubtless it would be puerile to pretend that typography had not made any material progress; it had done so in engraving and in composition; work was done more quickly, because the presses had been made more perfect. But the wise harmony of the old printers, their sure taste, even in their old irregular blocks, was no longer there to form a graceful and charming whole, which is to modern precision as a picture by Van Eyck is to a chromo-lithograph. Under Louis XIV., titles became regular, following, as we have said above, and modelling themselves on, the affected and peruked people who read them. All art entered on this path of sublimity and grandeur. The painter Le Brun is the highest exponent of this false Olympus, where an heroic pose became necessary for the most humble movements. Made popular by engraving by Pesne, Audran, Poilly, Edelinck, and a hundred others, this tendency overran everything: art and industry, painting and tapestry, illustration and typography itself. All was grand, in reverse of other times, when all was small and mean. The embellishments of the Book were full of gods in perukes and goddesses in armour, Louis XIV. as Apollo, as the sun illuminating the world. "Nec pluribus impar" was not the device of one man; it was the mighty and glorious cry of a whole people, from great to small, from the sublime painter to the modest printer.

Ordinarily these exaggerations are not useful to the arts. Here they were. But, for the matter that specially occupies us, it does not appear that the Book was much advanced. It approached a marvellous epoch of a delicate and graceful art; but it did not find its form; it dragged painfully after the Plantinian works, heavily throwing its etchings and burins in the middle of texts, gross and in bad taste. Yet taste in literature had an onward tendency; Molière and La Fontaine produced on their contemporaries the effect that in our day the naturalists have produced on the romanticists; but this was not for long. Majesty recovered its rights with Bossuet, Boileau, and the others.

JE laboure un champ plein d'épines
Qui ne rapporte fruit ny fleur,
Et me ſens piquer juſqu'au cœur
Par mille pointes aſſaſſines
Que mon deſtin à de malheur!
Ce n'eſt que labeur *&* douleur

Fig. 77.—Tailpiece of Sébastien Leclerc for the *Promenade de St. Germain*.

Sébastien Leclerc was one of the rare artists of the end of the seventeenth century who dreamed of the vignette in the midst of this invasion of pompous commonplace. Successor of Callot in manner, induced by the publishers, he began this style with a romance of La Calprenède, and continued with the *Promenade de St. Germain* of Louis le Laboureur, bailie of Montmorency, of whom Boileau said such curious things. This is one of the rarest books of Leclerc, and we reproduce one of the pages, with a charming tailpiece, which comes very near those of the eighteenth century. There was, moreover, a charm in this ingenious designer; he adorned the works of his contemporaries with graceful vignettes and decorations full of suppleness. It may be believed, besides, that he did not remain behind his *confrères* in figure composition or allegorical and Divine emblems. His art did not throw off the errors of the existing school; he was content not to copy any one and to make his works truly his own. Such were, for example, the vignettes of the *Histoire de Turenne*, where the heads of the chapters, the ornamented letters, and the tailpieces, harmoniously agree, and make the book, a little heavy in impression, a most agreeable work. Leclerc then found himself ready to design vignettes for the works of Racine for the publisher, Claude Barbin, another name frequently encountered in Boileau. The title of Vol. ii. merits attention.

The same year of this last publication, 1676, Sébastien Leclerc illustrated the "Metamorphoses" of Ovid for Benserade, the engraving of which cost the King more than 10,000 livres. Thus adorned, the book had not a bad appearance, but a satirist of the time, Hardin very probably, made on it this quatrain:—

"Mais quant à moi j'en trouve tout fort beau:
Papier, dorure, images, caractère,
Hormis les vers qu'il fallait laisser faire
"A La Fontaine."

It may be imagined what an engraver could produce working from 1650 and dying in 1715, that is, a life of work the longest that could be hoped for. Leclerc was the absolute contemporary of the King. He died, like him, at the beginning of the eighteenth century, leaving work widely scattered among books, funeral orations, and placards. After the example of Callot and Bosse, he did not disdain satire. One of his prettiest vignettes served to illustrate some pamphlet of Richesource against the journalists of his time; it represents a dandy of about 1679 offering his gazette.

By the side of this unrivalled antagonist it is permitted to place Lepautre, twenty years older than Leclerc, but whose studies had been principally on architecture. In the moments that he left his special work he devoted himself to frontispieces and vignettes; nevertheless, although he had before him the charming designs of Leclerc, he confined himself to a cold and hard manner, keeping, besides, as much as possible to titles, in which his particular talent could find scope. He designed also the Chartreux Missal of 1679, the *Gallia Christiana* after Marot, the *Dioptrique Oculaire* of P. Chérubin, engraved by Edelinck, and a thousand other works of small repute.

Fig. 78.—Small figure of Sébastien Leclerc for Richesource's pamphlet.

Very different was Francis Chauveau, who, without having the delicacy of Sébastien Leclerc or his art of arrangement, treated at least with grace little figures and illustrations. Certainly there is an enormous distance between these correct and commonplace engraved plates and the delightful wood engravings of the time of Geoffroy Tory, for example. But, be their worth what it may, they suited very well; and even with Molière they did not make such a bad figure. Chauveau was associated with many of the works of Leclerc, who caused him often to be less heavy, inasmuch as Leclerc corrected in engraving many of his compositions. It was so with Molière, and still more with Racine in the plate of the *Plaideurs*, in which Chauveau revealed himself a precursor of the eighteenth century. Unhappily he did not always follow this manner. Successively, and with various luck, he illustrated *Alaric*, *Andromaque*, and the "Metamorphoses" of Ovid for Benserade, with Leclerc; the *Pucelle* of Chapelain, and the *Tragédies* of Racine, to which Le Brun did not disdain to put his hand.

In short, the connecting link between the beginning of the seventeenth and that of the eighteenth century in the development of illustration is Sébastien Leclerc. He had known the artists of the first period; he was to see at his death appear one of the precursors of the vignettists of the following century, Claude Gillot. Thanks to him, overburdened titles and unskilful vignettes underwent a gradual transformation. In the delicacy and tenuity of his designs may be seen the dominant note of the eighteenth century, coquetry, and Choffard is divined. He was nearly the only one who did not fall into the exaggerations of the engravers of the time; he kept beside them without touching them, and preciously preserved his own well-accentuated personality. By the smallness and slenderness of his figures, Leclerc recalls somewhat the school of Fontainebleau; but he is above all the reflection of Callot, a Lorrainer like himself.

In Holland, a Frenchman, Bernard Picart, son of Stephen and pupil of Leclerc, was making a great name as an illustrator. He established himself as a print-seller at Amsterdam at the sign of "L'Etoile," and successively designed vignettes for many works, among others the Boileau of 1718. His vignettes and tailpieces, without possessing either the spirit of Leclerc or the grace of the eighteenth century, express an ingenious and inventive art that had broken with the strained traditions of preceding epochs.

From these two artists the decoration of the Book rapidly advanced. The form is found, and charming designers are not wanting to apply it.

The troubled state of England during the greater part of the seventeenth century no doubt accounts for the fact that the art of the Book made but very little progress. Theological controversies, the persecutions by the Puritans, and, above all, the great civil war and its antecedents and results, gave rise to a flood of publications of an ephemeral kind, which from their nature were hurriedly produced; and there was little room for pure literature and art. In the early part of the century, under the influence which Elizabeth left, and which James fostered, some important works were issued, with finely engraved illustrations; but wood engraving declined further and further, until it was artistically dead, to be revived in the next century. The works of the numerous poets and dramatists were printed in quarto, and collected editions of them in folio. Thus were issued the works of Shakespeare, first collected by Jaggard and Blount, 1623, folio, with an engraved portrait by Droeshout, the faithfulness of which was vouched in an opposite page of verse signed by Ben Jonson. "Don Quixote" first appeared in an English dress in 1612-20, published by E. Blount in quarto; and Jaggard, Blount's partner in the Shakespeare, published Boccaccio's "Decameron," in two volumes folio, 1620. Among other notable works of the early part of the century were Drayton's "Polyolbion," 1613; Chapman's Homer, 1611-15, folio, three volumes; Lord Bacon, whose essays and other single publications appeared in the seventeenth, to be collected as his "Works" in the next century; and William Prynne, whose *Histrio Mastrix*, 1633, so offended Charles I. by its references to the Queen and the court ladies, that the author had to undergo a severe and degrading punishment. Many of these works were illustrated with meritorious engravings on steel and copper by W. Hollar, P. Lombart, W. Marshall, Hole, W. Pass, W. Faithorne, and R. Vaughan. So that here were all the materials for the foundation of an English school, to be cruelly broken up shortly afterwards by the distractions of civil warfare.

In 1611 Robert Barker first printed the Authorised Version of the Holy Bible, which has been more often reprinted than any other book, and which exists to this day as the great standard of the English language.

The taste for books of travel which arose in the last century was largely increased by the voyages and discoveries of the English in North America and the subsequent Puritan exodus there. These early accounts of Virginia and New England, many of which are tracts of a few leaves only, now command fabulous prices. The great collection of voyages under the name of "Purchas: his Pilgrimes," was printed in five folio volumes, 1625-6, while De Bry, Hulsius, and Linschoten were enriching the world with their collections of travels, printed in Germany and Holland. All of these works were adorned with finely engraved plates, those to "Purchas" being engraved by Elstrack, and, besides, it had a famous map of the world, engraved by Hondius.

The controversial spirit engendered by the religious quarrels of the century and by the great civil war gave incessant work to the printers; and the many tracts and pamphlets thus produced were frequently illustrated by rude and coarse woodcuts, of no value from an artistic point of view, but curious from the indications they afford of the costumes and manners of the time.

The first edition of Walton's "Angler" was printed by R. Marriott in 1653, 16mo, with plates in the text, engraved on steel by Lombart. Butler's "Hudibras" appeared in 1663-78, and Milton's "Paradise Lost" in 1667, quarto. Fuller's "Worthies of England" was printed 1662, folio. We have roughly mentioned the principal English books of the century, and next approach the revival of literature and art in the eighteenth century.

CHAPTER V.

THE BOOK IN THE EIGHTEENTH CENTURY.

The regency—Publishers at the beginning of the eighteenth century—Illustrators in France; Gillot—The school of Watteau and Boucher—Cars—The younger Cochin; his principal works in vignettes—French art in England; Gravelot—Eisen—Choffard—The *Baisers* of Dorat; the *Contes* of La Fontaine—the publisher Cazin and the special literature of the eighteenth century—The younger Moreau and his illustrations—The Revolution—The school of David—Duplessis-Bertaux—The Book in Germany; Chodowiecki—In England; Boydell and French artists—Caslon and Baskerville—English books with illustrations—Wood engraving in the eighteenth century; the Papillons—Printing offices in the eighteenth century.

Fig. 79.—Letter by Cochin for the *Mémoires d' Artillerie* of Suvirey de St. Remy.

LIKE experience has shown us in our time, but in another manner, the beginning of the eighteenth century produced, in the manners and tastes of the French, an unconscious but tenacious reaction. It seemed as if the conceptions of romanticism had lasted long enough, and that the cycle of Middle Age chevaliers had passed away, and that a return to what is called nature was effected in literature and art. At the death of Louis XIV., Olympus and its gods, majestic poses and suns, had become wearisome. By a little half-open door, gaiety escaped from its prison and fled. For the Book that door was the hand of Sébastien Leclerc.

The ancient school was replaced. Constrained during three quarters of a century, French manners began to be joyous under the regency of the Duc d'Orleans. If the representatives of another age still lived, if Rigaud always painted his portraits in peruke, there were new-comers, enlivened by the new fashions, less solemn and more bewitching. Le Brun was then far in the past, and as amusing to the ladies of the regency as are now to us the fashions of the Second Empire.

The Book, after its manner, followed the movement, and gradually found the elements of its decoration in the tendencies of the day. Small sizes were multiplied, types showed elegance, and vignettes became more and more agreeable and intellectual. Amateurs had their *ex-libris* engraved. The smallest pamphlets were covered with ornamental letters, vignettes, and tailpieces, already very clever. Costume also, in its shorter and lighter form, gave to designers a means of agreeably composing a page of illustration and disseminating fancy in the figures. These revolutions worked themselves simply from day to day, as taste became more pronounced and exacting.

The commerce of the Book was still extending from the end of the preceding century; and if the number of printers was limited and arrested by certain somewhat hard laws, production in Paris was enormous. Among regulations that weighed most heavily on publishers figured the obligation put upon them by the ordinance of 1713 to deposit eight copies of illustrated books. In 1725 the King issued other regulations to affirm the rights of the university against the corporation, forcing the masters to assist in a body at the processions of the Sorbonne and to offer on the Day of the Purification a candle to the rector. In spite of this ordinance, more religious than useful to commerce, the fashion of vignettes increased. The principal shops were searched, as they are still, for novelties; the Rue St. Jacques and the Quai des Augustins, where they were grouped, were resorted to. The most important booksellers in 1727 were Coignard, the Barbous—who essayed afterwards, with Lengley Dufresnoy, to copy the Elzevirs,—Cavalier, Robustel, Fournier, Ballard, and D'Houry. Of the two last, D'Houry printed the calendars, and Ballard had the privilege for music. Another, Leonord, published the books of the Dauphin. At these and other publishers', recent works were examined, those who did not buy gave their advice and took ideas, and so fashion slowly formed itself. It was thus that Houdart de la Motte published with G. Dupuis in 1719 a collection of fables, with illustrations of Claude Gillot, which was the talk at the booksellers'.

In this book all was original: the author, who had had, five years before, the eccentric idea of translating the Iliad without knowing a word of Greek; the text, a kind of imitation of La Fontaine, without salt or savour; the size, quarto, admirably printed by Dupuis, in the Rue St. Jacques, with plates by Coypel, Massé, and, above all, the charming vignettes of Gillot, the most pleasing and clever of all his collaborators, a sort of Callot fallen into the eighteenth century, and who ought to take the first place by birthright. Gillot has been called, not without reason, "the last pagan of the Renaissance;" and this pagan had the honour to give us Watteau.

Fig. 80.—Vignette by Gillot for the *Chien et le Chat*, fable by Houdart de la Motte, in 1719.

The Count de Caylus tells the story. Gillot had quitted the pencil for the etching needle on seeing the work of his pupil. He had no reason to complain; his pictures were of no value, and his prints gave other artists the idea of imitating them. The whole French school of the eighteenth century may have had its origin in this forgotten book, illustrated by the master of Watteau. In fact, in the manner of the little etching here given we may easily perceive the coquetry and affectation that were later the dominant tone of vignettes. For, it may well be said, the graceful, feminine, and arch manner of which we speak was, above all, conventional and false. In opposition to the designers and engravers of the fifteenth and beginning of the sixteenth century, who reproduced naturally scenes of daily life in ideal conceptions, it came, through the moral education of the artists, that they put forth the ideal in the most ordinary things of life. Shepherds were no longer the gross, rustic peasants that we find in primitive Flemish paintings or in the "Hours" of Simon Vostre; they were coxcombs, pomaded and adorned with ribbons, playing the bagpipes, and making love to the shepherdesses of the court.

At first it was Watteau who influenced all the engravers in the pretty and the smart; Boucher did the rest; and fatally the Book followed, and followed impetuously, surpassing, if possible, the painted works. If the severe poses, the grave touch, of the preceding century are no longer found, they often go a little far in the contrary sense. It may be well said here that the arts are ordinarily the result of the manners of an epoch. The system of Law was not without influence on the entire eighteenth century, by the terrible manner in which he upset fortunes, awoke appetites, gave rein to aspirations hitherto held in check. Claude Gillot, the designer, was one of the first victims of the Scotch banker; he lost his fortune on the Exchange; but who may say what his artistic ambition dreamed of in the midst of all these disorders? One thing is certain: that Watteau, his pupil, broke off very short with the style of the seventeenth century.

Laurent Cars was the engraver who multiplied the compositions of Boucher, and made them the fashion. He engraved also, after the painter of shepherds and nymphs, illustrations to Molière, the most agreeable that there are for style and spirit. In engraving certain works of Lemoyne, Cars did not completely desert the ancient school. He appears at the beginning of the eighteenth century as if divided between two manners each equally possible to him.

The work of these engravers was almost exclusively in etching, biting with acid a copper plate covered with varnish, on which the drawing was made by means of a point. This process, always previously used for sketches, served also for finishing vignettes, which up to then had been finished by the burin.

The suppleness of the work was greater, and the artist remained more himself than he could be with the stiff cutting instrument of the seventeenth century.

The sizes of books had not yet all come to octavo or duodecimo. The works of Molière published by Prault in 1734 in six volumes quarto, under the direction of Marc Antoine Joly, give the idea of an important work, not at all of theatrical pieces. To tell the truth, these somewhat exaggerated dimensions allow artists more room for illustration; later, when smaller forms predominated, text and engravings were so compressed that they were not always clear and readable to every eye; but the quarto was not graceful, it was not in harmony with the finikin, the pastoral pieces, then presented, and it had to disappear as a current size in illustrated publications.

The class of artisans employed on the Book is not identical in the eighteenth century with that of printers and publishers. In the beginning, as we have seen, the cutters of wood blocks and the printers were often the same people, preparing their characters or their blocks, and afterwards putting them under the press. Large printing offices had very quickly changed that. Each particular work had its special workman. Typography had its type-founders, compositors, forwarders, inkers, and pressmen. In the eighteenth century this was complicated by designers, engravers, plate-printers, and these different professions occupied themselves on the Book in manipulating the sheets in their turn. In the midst of this crowd, the designers and engravers, esteemed as was their collaboration, were not the most honoured. Their homes often reflected the effect of their life as clever artists, quick to spend the money earned during the week; and we shall have occasion to name some of the more miserable among them.

The booksellers, on the contrary, had become great personages. In the preceding chapter we have seen Cramoisy and Vitré, to name only them, acquire the greatest honours, the latter painted by Philip de Champagne, with many others lords of the court. In the eighteenth century there were Brunet, Ballard, Mariette, Chardon, Didot, and a host of others, during the time of Watteau, Boucher, and Cars, of which we shall shortly speak; and these several publishers had houses of their own, and furnished shops and printing offices with the best apparatus. Saved from falling into negligences by royal regulations on printing, they composed with admirable characters, on paper of the first order, imperishable works; and, usual consequence of their high situation, they paid the artists badly charged with their work. It would be long and tedious to enter into this matter in detail. They made progress by slow degrees, and in good time they marvellously united copper plate engraving to printed text, so marvellously, that in comparing their works to the wood blocks of the sixteenth century, it may be asked which of the two styles is superior in elegance and good taste.

Fig. 81.—Vignette for *Daphnis et Chloe* by Cochin, for Coustelier's edition.

One of the ancestors of this group of vignettists was the younger Cochin, who had engraved the plate of the monks in the fables of Houdart, illustrated by Gillot. Cochin, in spite of his passion for allegory and his very marked taste for affectation, gave, it may be said, with the designer-engraver St. Aubin, an enormous impulse to the art of adorning books. From the beginning of his career he worked for the publishers, composing frontispieces, ornamented letters, and tailpieces, or transferring to copper the drawings of others. Singular type of artist, besides, educated, well brought up, epicurean and spendthrift, friend of great lords, and protected by Madame de Pompadour. When he travelled in Italy with her young brother Abel Poisson, Cochin did everything, was ready at the least request, inventing curious menus, giving representations of fêtes, and yet finding the time to decorate books and design vignettes profusely.

He worked chiefly for Jombert, a sort of learned bookseller, King's printer for the artillery, who dates from July, 1736. Jombert was visited by painters. He gave little private soirées, which Cochin attended, and where he daily made numerous friends. It was in this house, of so special a character, and, it may be said, so little artistic at first sight, that Cochin invented his best frontispieces, among them that of the *Calcul Différentiel*, that of the *Astronomie Physique*, and the plates of the *Méthode de Dessin*, after Boucher. He was one of the first to produce engraved titles, with which the publisher Prault ornamented his dainty volumes, and which were imitated, up to the end of the eighteenth century, by all the illustrators who followed. In that to the works of Madame Deshoulières the letter itself is engraved. Since then the open letter has been copied in typography. These vignettes were used many times by publishers, sometimes simply effacing the inscription, sometimes reproducing the original design by a different artist. The boy with the swan had decorated in 1744 a "Jerusalem Delivered" in Italian, by the same publisher, Prault; it was then engraved by Aveline. Fessard engraved the second plate, which is here reproduced.

ŒUVRES
de Me et Mlle
DESHOULIERES
Nouvelle Edition
TOME PREMIER
A PARIS
Chez Prault fils Quay de Conty

Fig. 82.—Title-page engraved by Fessard after Cochin for the works of Madame Deshoulières, 1747.

Nearly all the frontispieces of the Book with vignettes of the eighteenth century preserve this arrangement: an ornamented and draped border, with garlands of roses, symbols, and cupids, in the middle the title, in red and black, composed in open letter, often a scroll with the address of the publisher, but rarely a mark. It was the time of little winged cupids, goddesses, and gods. The goddesses were the favourites of the kings, Madame de Pompadour or the princesses, but rarely the virtuous Marie Leczinska, too homely and too much ignored to tempt the artists; the kings or the princes were the gods.

After Jombert, Prault, and Coustellier, Cochin worked for François Didot, syndic of the printers, for whom he prepared a set of illustrations to Molière. Unfortunately Didot died in 1757, and the project fell with him. Of the work of Cochin there only remains the set of *Tartufe* etchings in octavo.

In the vortex into which he was plunged, he successively illustrated the works of Rousseau, published at Brussels, quarto; those of Boileau, published by David and Durand, octavo; and Henault's "History of France," in the same size, with numerous vignettes. One of these should be noted in a book treating of printing; it is that in which Cochin pretends to show to his contemporaries the interior of a workshop in 1470. Without doubt the sketch of this print was taken in one of the houses frequented by him—at Jombert's, Didot's, or David and Durand's—for that room in which compositors are working and printed sheets drying was not an invention of Cochin, and served to reproduce a printing office of the eighteenth century.

Fig. 83.—Vignette taken from P. Corneille's *Théâtre*, by Gravelot.

With Cochin soon worked a number of designers and aqua-fortists, too prudent to lose the opportunity. The fashion arrived for books beribboned, festooned, and flowered. Hubert François Gravelot had carried to London this style of new works, which he knew how to decorate, in his manner, better than any one, with letters, figures, and tailpieces. He did not engrave much himself, leaving this work to lesser artists, and contenting himself with subtle invention and graceful subjects. With Eisen, Cochin, and Moreau, he is the French artist in the sense of the time, free, bold, and ingenious, but perhaps a little out of place in England. He published his plates to the "Decameron" in 1757, one of the most curious of his sets of plates, and a hundred various vignettes. On his return to France he designed the *Théâtre* of P. Corneille, from which the *Galerie de Palais* is here reproduced, on account of the illustration of bookselling which it gives. In 1764 the large *salon* of the Palace was still, as in the time of Abraham Bosse, a place where shops were fitted up and the new books discussed. Side by side with the dressmakers and merchants of every category, the bookseller offers to his customer the recent products of Parisian presses. Certain works were sold under cover and not shown; there is here something to pique the curiosity of unoccupied young men who strolled about and prolonged their stay in the galleries.

Fig. 84.—Border designed by Choffard in 1758.

Eisen has a simplicity, a good taste, and a special and singularly perfect economy of artistic effect combined with typography. It appears hard that the designer had no consultative voice in the choice of impression and disposition of the Book. The union of the two forces, the vignette and the composition, is so close that it may be believed one was made for the other, neither venturing to assert itself. In the pretty and elaborate inventions of the artists reigned a lackadaisical affectation that was delightfully becoming; the rock-work, which it still had, suited admirably the borders of the first page. The *Lettres d'une Peruvienne* has a very agreeable title, but little different, on the whole, from that of Madame Deshoulières, by Cochin. It is the same with the *Lettres Turques*, published at Amsterdam in 1750, and generally in all the frontispieces signed by him. As to the other decorations of the Book, there were also a number of ingenious artists, confusing cupids and flowers, imposing blazons, delighting in playing with accumulated difficulties. Under this assuredly involuntary but real direction, publications attained proportions of luxury and coquetry until then unknown. The volume of *Baisers* of Dorat would not have lived but for Eisen and the delightful fancies with which he adorned it.

At the same time, we find Choffard, another designer and etcher of much repute, and sought after by the booksellers. Under his pencil the vignette became a *chef-d'œuvre*, the tailpiece was a delightful compound of judicious and sportive ornament, the taste for which grew more and more. From delicate foliage are suspended roses, shepherds' pipes, lyres, and zithers. With the zephyrs scrolls or ribbons float, carried by winged cupids. The initial letters are real pictures, of such fineness and precision that the difficulties of their reproduction prevent us from putting them before the reader.

When the *fermiers généraux*, those great amateur financiers of the last century, conceived the idea of an edition of the *Contes* of La Fontaine at their expense, their eyes naturally fell upon the artists best prepared to illustrate the inimitable fancies of the great poet, Eisen and Choffard. The first had for his task the composition of the plates, Choffard the general decoration. Ficquet was added for the portrait of the *bonhomme* La Fontaine—Ficquet, whose specialty in this *genre* was dazzling in its delicacy and spirit; Diderot wrote a short introduction; the composition was confided to a printer of the first order, and it was put on sale by Barbou.

Fig. 85.—Vignette by Eisen for the Quiproquo in the Contes of La Fontaine, in the edition of the fermiers généraux.

It is not a book to be recommended from a moral point of view, but the typographical art, joined to that of designers and engravers, never obtained a more complete success: the size in octavo, the impression clear, united with the dimensions of the plates in a harmonious elegance, well calculated to please the three rich personages and the joyous amateurs to whom the *Contes* address themselves. True, Eisen has dressed the greater part of the characters in the costume of his time, which is a little hurtful to one's feelings to-day; it may be imagined, however, that it was La Fontaine who was mistaken, so that these delicate, risky tales appear to be created for the seigneurs of the time of Louis XV.

All the special literature sought for then by rich people had not the value of the *Contes*. There was at Rheims a person, who has to-day become the *mode*, as he was in the time of Louis XVI., who sold under cover a quantity of licentious books of the better kind, adorned with figures by Eisen, Marillier, or Cochin; this was Cazin, an artist in his way, but whose good name suffered under a scandalous trial. An order of the Council of State in 1764 enjoined him to cease his trade in the Place Royale at Rheims, where he sold his particular merchandise. It appears that the sentence was not without appeal, for we find Cazin at Paris about 1785. He was one of those who were ruined by the Revolution, after he had popularised the editions known as *Petits Formats*, printed by Valade, of Paris.

Fig. 86.—Card of the publisher Prault, uncle by marriage of Moreau le Jeune.

We have come to the most beautiful illustrated books of the eighteenth century, and to the illustrious artists of whom we shall speak in good time should be added the younger Moreau and St. Aubin, the former nephew by marriage of the publisher Prault, and therefrom a decorator of the Book, the other thrown by Gravelot into full work, and rapidly becoming the most subtle and adroit of the etchers of the time. Moreau did not wait long after his marriage before setting to work. He began with ornaments destined for the *Histoire de France* of President Henault; then he composed, in his own personal manner, titles and tailpieces for his uncle. In the Book he is the propagator of garlands of roses, which he grouped with an ideal grace; he twined them in the borders of his frontispieces, and put them judiciously in his tailpieces. He excelled in inventing subjects referring to the text which were not commonplace ornaments suitable for anything. The tailpiece on p. 202, taken from the works of Molière, brings forcibly to mind the *Médecin malgre Lui*, with its wood-cutter unmercifully beaten with sticks and muffled in a scientific robe. It is the same with other illustrations, that cannot be displaced from the position assigned to them by the artist without disappointment.

Fig. 87.—Tailpiece from the *Médecin malgre Lui*, by Moreau le Jeune.

The year 1773, which saw the publication by De Bret of the works of Molière, may perhaps be considered as that in which the French Book of the eighteenth century reached its culminating point. M. de Laborde, first valet de chambre of the King and governor of the Louvre, published with De Lormel, printer to the Academy of Music, his celebrated collection of *Chansons*, dedicated to the young Dauphiness Marie Antoinette, and partly illustrated by the younger Moreau. The work is exquisite, of powerful yet simple grace. The sentimental note of the century was struck in it, the insipid love of shepherdesses there tenderly sighed, and the designer has delightfully rendered this arch side of the pastoral song.

Our task does not permit us to linger over the works of this prodigious and charming artist, but we must mention his inimitable plates to J. J. Rousseau, the finest and most agreeable of his compositions and vignettes, also his *chef-d'œuvre*, the *Histoire du Costume*.

Fig. 88.—Vignette of the "Pardon Obtenu," designed by Moreau le Jeune, for Laborde's *Chansons*, in 1773.

As evidencing the activity of French artists of the Book in the eighteenth century, we cite the number of works illustrated by the respective artists enumerated in the last edition of M. H. Cohen's valuable *Guide de l'Amateur de Livres à Gravures du XVIIIe Siècle*:—

Aliamet, 34.
Audran, 16.
Aveline, 33.
Baquoy, 87.
Basan, 9.
Binet, 48.
Borel, 29.
Boucher, 47.
Bovinet, 34.
Cars, 13.
Chedel, 21.
Chenu, 18.

Massard, 40.
Monnet, 67.
Monsiau, 22.
Moreau, 138.
Née, 48.
Pasquier, 18.
Patas, 65.
Pauquet, 23.
Petit, 23.
Picart, 62.
Ponce, 65.
Prévost, 40.
Prud'hon, 14.
Queverdo, 54.
Rigaud, 18.
Roger, 17.
Romanet, 26.
Rousseau, 24.
St. Aubin, 70.
Scotin, 27.
Sève, 29.
Simonet, 83.
Tardieu, 64.
Tilliard, 15.
Trière, 39.

Doubtless some of these ascriptions are for frontispieces only, but as a list of the principal book illustrators of the time, and as showing the measure of their popularity, this table is of much interest.

With the Revolution the decline of the Book arrives, as that of all the arts. Moreau, friend of David, had become affected by the new ideas and the burlesque renaissance of Greek and Roman art. He made his apology on the altar of the gods, and engraved portraits on wood to punish himself for having painted the elegancies of fallen tyrants. At this game, nerve, as well as suppleness, was lost; and if he had had only the artistic knack of the Revolution, his daughter, married to Charles Vernet, could not have written of him, "That which can be most admired is, at the same time, the fecundity and flexibility of Moreau's talent, that marvellous facility of conceiving a picturesque scene and disposing it in an interesting and truthful manner in the least extended space." This was true before, but after?

In spite of his passion for the ideas and men of the Revolution, Moreau found himself at the end of his resources. Renouard, the publisher, received him as he had received St. Aubin, to whom he advanced sum after sum to prevent him dying of hunger. Like most of his contemporaries, Moreau, pressed by want, "took, quitted, and retook the cuirass and the hair-shirt." He had drawn for everybody: for Louis XVI., for the Republic, for Napoleon I.

The worst of it is that after his designs for Ovid, Molière, and Rousseau, dating from the reign of Louis XVI., he should have done them again in 1804, 1806, and 1808. The difference was great, even probably for his publishers, Renouard and Dupréel. It does not appear that the pontiff of the new school, David, knew of his distress; and Moreau succumbed in 1814 to a cancerous scirrhus of the right arm, forgotten and in the greatest misery.

We have passed a little quickly to the end of the century because it is of no importance to name each of the publishers and artists, but only to sketch briefly their tastes or their manner. We have not dwelt long on the engravers so called, because of their number; but their dexterity remains proverbial; they handled etching with extreme suppleness, and often interpreted the drawings of illustrators in remitting them to the needle. Many of these, not to say all, made use themselves of the etching needle, St. Aubin for example, who knew how to give to the work of others his personal mark and distinction.

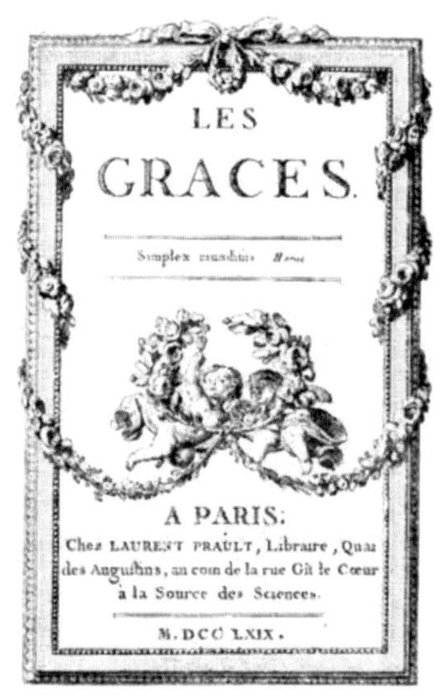
LES

GRACES.

Simplex munditiis Horat.

A PARIS:

Chez LAURENT PRAULT, Libraire, Quai des Augustins, au coin de la rue Gît le Cœur à la Source des Sciences.

M.DCC LXIX.

Fig. 89.—Title designed by Moreau le Jeune in 1769 for the publisher Prault.

The Revolution passed over some among those that it ruined, and, as stated above, they followed the movement, and lost themselves in the school of

David. It was Duplessis-Bertaux who, after having furnished to Cazin, the publisher, vignettes for his *Recueil des Meilleurs Contes en Vers*, 1778, and many other books, after having worked for Didot, devoted himself to patriotic engraving and to the reproduction of scenes of the Revolution. When he published his *Tableaux Historiques*, in three volumes folio, adorned with nearly two hundred large plates, it was under the Consulate, that is to say far from the time when the work was begun. Renouvier assures us, with his exclusive disdain for the eighteenth century, that Duplessis-Bertaux was a mystifier, and that his scenes of the Revolution were a hoax, "in the kind of spirit in vogue under the Directory." The truth is that the artist, in place of being a cheerful Callot, as might be thought from his manner of engraving, so like that of the Lorraine artist, was imbued with the emphatic and exaggerated impressions of the first Republic, its *sans-culottes* in the poses of the Sabines and its *tricoteuses* apeing Penelope.

The immense artistic advance made in France in the eighteenth century in the manufacture and illustration of the Book made itself felt throughout Europe. In Germany, Chodowiecki, born at Dantzic of a family of apothecaries, developed his talent from ornamenting the boxes of his father, and from 1758 to 1794 he designed numerous plates for books and almanacs, a little heavy in engraving, but singularly clever in composition. There were a few others also designing, and Kilian, Folkema, and Ridinger produced some fine engravings, but the Book did not make so much progress in Germany as in France and England.

In England a vast improvement was manifested. Fine types were cast by Baskerville and Caslon; printing machines were perfected. The illustration of books by engraved plates was in the first half of the century almost entirely done by foreigners, but an English school was arising, which attained perfection in the latter half of the eighteenth and first half of the nineteenth century. Wood engraving also, which, with the exception of blocks for head and tailpieces, had become almost a lost art, was revived by Bewick, to become later one of the chief adornments of the Book.

Before 1716 English printers obtained their best founts of type from Holland, but the establishment of the Caslon foundry rendered them independent. William Caslon, the first great English type-founder, was born 1692, and died 1766. The foundry still exists, pre-eminent in the beauty of its characters. Baskerville established a foundry about 1750, and printed at Birmingham with his own types a number of extremely beautiful books. The impetus given to fine printing by these two men rapidly spread itself, and laid the foundation of the perfection which English book-making reached.

As mentioned above, Gravelot illustrated many English books in the early part of the century. He designed a set of plates to Shakespeare in 12mo, 1740, and another in quarto, 1744, besides numerous frontispieces and other plates in all kinds of books. Among other foreigners who engraved for English publishers were Grignion, Kip, Van der Gucht, Houbraken, and Bartolozzi. Bartolozzi, who was very prolific in the production of engraved plates, may perhaps be called the founder of that great English school of engraving which arose with the establishment of the Royal Academy in 1769 and the encouragement given by Alderman Boydell. Houbraken and Vertue engraved a set of fine portraits in folio for Rapin's "History of England," 1736; William Hogarth designed plates for Butler's "Hudibras," 1744; and among other curiosities of English engraving before 1750 were Sturt's edition of the Common Prayer, entirely engraved on copper plates, 1717, and an edition of Horace entirely engraved by Pine, 1733. That the taste for illustrated books soon grew to be great is evidenced by the publication of such expensive works as Boydell's edition of Shakespeare, in nine volumes folio, commenced in 1791, and adorned with a hundred plates from pictures specially commissioned by the spirited publisher; Claude's *Liber Veritatis*, with three hundred engravings by Richard Earlom 1777, Sir Robert Strange's engravings of fifty historical prints about 1750, collections of views in Great Britain by Kip, Buck, and Boydell; Holbein's "Collection of Portraits" 1792, a hundred and fifty plates to Shakespeare engraved by S. and E. Harding 1793, all of which cost great sums to produce, and greatly contributed to the elevation of public taste. Among the artists of the latter half of the century who contributed to the decoration of the Book are Thomas Stothard, whose very beautiful designs, extending into the next century, excelled those of all his contemporaries in their grace and spirit; Robert Smirke, best known by his plates for Shakespeare, "Don Quixote," and "Gil Blas;" Burney; and Richard Westall. It may be said generally that the English books of the eighteenth century were of a more solid character than the French, although English art, especially in the decoration of the Book, owes much to French initiation. It is curious to read now the opinion of a contemporary French engraver on English art. Choffard, in the preface to Basan's *Dictionnaire* 1767, wrote, "They" (the English), "having been supported by some foreign talent, are trying to create talent among themselves; but they have not seized the flame of genius that vivifies all art in France."

Fig. 90.—Tailpiece engraved on wood by John Baptist Papillon (before 1766).

However, what had become of engraving by cutting in reverse, the figure in relief, from which printing could be done? It had, we may think, nearly disappeared in the midst of the continued invasion of the burin and etching. It only appeared from time to time in head and tailpieces, remaining purely typographical and lost in other decorations. There were always wood engravers, not very clever, capable only of working simple lines without charm. One of them resolved to resuscitate the art, and made various attempts about the end of the reign of Louis XIV. and beginning of that of Louis XV. He was named John Papillon, and was born at St. Quentin in 1661. His experiments did not go beyond a book of prayers, with thirty-six figures in relief after Sébastien Leclerc. His son, John Baptist, succeeded him, and continued to engrave without ceasing subjects of ornament, letters, often tailpieces, of a good style upon the whole, and taking an excellent place in an elaborate book. Unfortunately, grace had fled; the processes that the practitioners exhibited one after the other were lost; and the Papillons reconstituted, we may say, a vanished art. John Baptist also published in 1766 a theoretical treatise on wood engraving, abounding in historical errors, but in which something to learn may be found if taken with discernment. He says in his preface, "Now that excellent work is done on copper, wood engraving is neglected, and the use lost of designing and cutting the shadows of the pencil on the wood block; most of those who work in it have neither design nor taste, and only follow their own ideas; it is not astonishing that only very mediocre pieces come from their hands, to say nothing stronger; the profound ignorance of nearly all who meddle with it contrives more and more to destroy the beauties of this art in which many people find neither pleasure nor grace. To obviate all this, if it be possible to me, I have undertaken to give my precepts and observations to those who wish to apply themselves to my engraving."

It was probably the essays of Papillon that provoked curious experiments on the part of other wood engravers. Duplat, at the beginning of this century, proposed to prepare a relief on stone, and as this would be broken under pressure, he invented a mould; that is to say, he took a leaden matrix from the stone cutting, and ran a resistant metal into this mould, thus obtaining a relief similar to the stone. Renouard, the publisher, made the trials; and the younger Moreau made the designs. Moreau become an essayer of processes in 1811! One of the plates of La Fontaine's *Fables*, published by Renouard in 1812, in two volumes, 12mo, is here reproduced.

Fig. 91.—Experiment in engraving in relief by Moreau le Jeune for Renouard's edition of La Fontaine's *Fables*.

It appears, however, that the publisher was thwarted by bad printing. The printers of Didot or Mame, much as they consecrated all their care to it, did not yet know perfect workmanship; they put the most intense blacks into fine sheets. The great publishers trusted that better days would leave to more clever men the task of perfecting the invention.

Fig. 92.—Portrait of Thomas Bewick.

Wood engraving owes its revival and almost perfection in England to Thomas Bewick, who published his first work in 1770, his "General History of Quadrupeds" 1790, and his "Birds" 1797. In these works he not only depicted his subjects with the most scrupulous fidelity, but in the tailpieces of the several chapters he drew the most quaint, humorous, and faithful representations of country life. He, with his brother, John Bewick, and their pupils, among whom was Luke Clennell, had an influence upon English art and the decoration of the Book in England which exists to our day. Not alone with us, for he may be said to have repaid the debt which we owed to France for her illustrated books of the eighteenth century by stimulating the art of wood engraving, which was practised by Tony Johannot and the other illustrators of the nineteenth century.

To return to the eighteenth century, with which this chapter is specially occupied, we have said that the Royal Printing House, after various fortunes, still existed; and in 1788 it worked, for better or for worse, at the Louvre. According to the budget of that year, it cost the King 90,000 livres, of which the director had 1,400.

There were, on the other hand, a certain number of official printing offices, that of war, for example, which was devoted entirely to the work of the Ministry. It was situated at Versailles, and was created in 1768. It is told of Louis XV. that, being one day in this workshop, he found a pair of spectacles, left as if in inadvertence on a printed sheet. As his sight was weakening, he took the spectacles and looked through them. The sheet was a hyperbolical eulogium composed, as if at random, by the director Bertier, in honour of the King. Louis XV., having read the dithyramb, replaced the spectacles, and quietly said, "They are too strong; they make objects too large."

Who would believe that at the end of the century of Voltaire and Rousseau a craftsman would be found desirous of leading back the typographical art to its cradle, and of making xylographs again, under the name of polytypes? A German was the original who conceived the plan. He obtained an order of council for the establishment of his presses in 1785, but the same council suppressed them 1st November, 1787. His process was to substitute for movable characters a plate of fixed letters, and probably engraved.

Another eccentricity of typography at the end of the century was the introduction of "logography" by John Walter, the proprietor and printer of the *Times* newspaper, which consisted in casting whole the words in most common use, in place of separate letters. The system had soon to be abandoned, but the early numbers of the *Times*, which was started January 1st, 1785, were printed on it.

In the eighteenth century there was a printing establishment for each of the constituted bodies; the King, the Queen, the princes, each had their own. The royal lottery occupied a special printing house.

The young inmates of the blind asylum worked under the direction of M. Clousier, royal printer. Louis XVI. authorised the celebrated Haüy, their master, to allow them to print; and in 1786 they composed an essay on the education of the blind. Pierre François Didot was in 1785 printer to the Prince, afterwards Louis XVIII.; and he published the *Aventures de Télémaque*, in two quarto volumes, from this special printing office.

The English colonies in North America early established printing there, their first book, the "Book of Psalms," known as the Bay Psalm Book, being dated 1640. By the middle of the eighteenth century literature held a strong position in the colonies, the greater part of it being, as might be expected, English; but the revolution and subsequent establishment of the United States created a national American literature, which has flourished to this day. Among the printers of North America in the eighteenth century, the most famous was the celebrated philosopher Dr. Benjamin Franklin, who served his apprenticeship to the printing press in London. He returned to America in 1726, and worked as a printer with his brother at Philadelphia.

CHAPTER VI.

THE BOOK IN THE NINETEENTH CENTURY.

The Didots and their improvements—The folio Racine—The school of Didot—Fine publications in England and Germany—Literature and art of the Restoration—Romanticism—Wood engraving—Bewick's pupils, Clennell, etc.—The illustrators of romances—The generation of 1840—The Book in our days in Europe and America.

P OLITICAL imitators had not been found for the French Revolution in all the neighbouring countries of Europe, but its Greco-Roman art established itself, and by degrees was introduced into the studios of painters and the printing offices. Prud'hon, Gerard, Girodet, and later Desenne, without counting the younger Moreau and his contemporaries of the older regime, rallied to the new study, forming a school of illustrators and vignettists with which the publishers could resolutely advance. England followed suit with Flaxman, West, Fuseli, Barry, and a crowd of others. Among the publishers the powerful family of the Didots took first rank, and its members, at once type-founders, printers, booksellers, and *savants* of the first order, were the best fitted to direct an artistic and literary movement. When Napoleon crowned himself emperor of the French, the elders of the family had already brought about a number of perfections and discoveries in their profession by which their workshops had profited. François Ambroise, who died in the year of the Empire, had given an exact proportion to types, a free and elegant turn, but perhaps too regular and precise to be agreeable. He had also invented a press called the *presse à un coup*, in which the impression was taken by a single pull instead of being produced by a series of successive strikings. His brother, Pierre François, spoken of in the preceding chapter, was a type-founder and paper-maker at Essones, and counted among his official titles "printer to the Comte de Provence," as François Ambroise was to the Comte d'Artois.

Of these two branches equally faithful to typography, Pierre Didot, son of François Ambroise, became the head on the death of his father. Born in 1760, he had studied his art with passion, and had merited the installation of his workshops in the Louvre, where he published a celebrated collection known as the Louvre editions, the *chef-d'œuvre* of which was the works of Racine. The splendid execution of this book, in three large folio volumes, was a true typographical revolution. Never in any country had scrupulous perfection of detail been joined to so masterly a knowledge of disposition and form of characters. The great artists of the Davidian school had the honour of seeing their drawings reproduced as illustrations, and those named above designed the fifty-seven plates with which the edition was adorned. Pierre Didot displayed a great affectation in only printing two hundred and fifty copies of his irreproachable and marvellous work, of which a hundred had proofs of the plates before letters. Published by subscription, the ordinary edition was issued at 1,200 francs, and with proofs 1,800 francs.

To these superb works Firmin Didot, his brother, added ingenious discoveries. Struck with certain difficulties of printing as well as of correction, he imagined the welding together of the types of a forme, when once obtained without faults, so as to avoid the trouble of new composition. This process, useless for books of small number, had a capital importance in the case of reimpressions of popular and successful works. He named this method stereotype, and from 1799 he published a Racine in 18mo by this method; but the originality of the method, which he was the first to call stereotype, ended with its name, for the process had already been discovered by William Ged, a goldsmith of Edinburgh, in 1725, the first book produced in this manner being an edition of Sallust, printed in 1744, 8vo, "non typis mobilibus ut vulgo fieri solet, sed tabellis seu laminis fusis, excudebat."

This admirably directed house, we may indeed say this school of typography, formed with Renouard, Claye, Rignoux, and others, the greater number of the French publishers of the middle of the century. When the Czar Alexander went to Paris, he wished to do honour to the greatest French practitioners in the science of printing, in the persons of the brothers Pierre and Firmin Didot. But these were not the only ones. The sons of Pierre François, Henri and Pierre François II.—the latter specially applied himself to paper-making, under the name of Didot St. Leger—followed in the footsteps of their father and uncle.
Pierre François made at Essones an excellent paper, which he brought to the perfection of making it in endless rolls, such as are made to-day for rotary machines. Bernardin de St. Pierre retired to Essones about the end of the last century, and there married the daughter of Pierre François II. It is a curious coincidence that the same village contained at once the man whose works at the beginning of the century had so extraordinary a success and the great family of printers who had given definitive impetus to typographical work. It was in this tranquil circle that the author of "Paul and Virginia," at the age of sixty, sought repose; that the publication of his book was resolved upon with all the luxury due to its success, with admirable type and with plates by Prud'hon and others. He added to it the *Chaumière Indienne*, written in 1790, on the eve of the Terror, which is one of the most delicate novels of the time.

The homely and sweet literature of Bernardin de St. Pierre, the heroic inventions of Girodet, Gerard, and Chaudet in the Greek or Roman style, the clever but severe typography of the Didots—such is the composition of the Book at the beginning of the century, and also its avowed tendency and good taste. Under Louis XV. the nymphs carried panniers; Polyeucte had peruke and sword. It would be unbecoming not to give Juno or Venus the head-dress adopted in paintings and vignettes. At the time which now occupies us fashion in clothing directed designers also. The hair of goddesses was *à la Titus*; the waist was under the arms; golden circles were on the brow. Simple mortals walked naked on the roads, with plumed casques and superb shields. There were heroes putting forth their disproportioned arms, others raising their eyes to heaven in impossible attitudes. Such were all the vignettes, from Girodet to the humblest, the last, the most forgotten.

It happens, by an oddity of which the cause is vainly sought, that this classic and revolutionary school of David identifies itself so well with the Napoleonic epoch, then with the people of the Restoration, that it seems expressly made for them. At the same time, under Louis XVIII. and Charles X. the Romans and Greeks had not the bold carriage of their early days; they became more citizenised, and assumed the air of the national guards of the kingdom of which later an excessive use was made.

England also had a splendid series of publishers and printers. From Boydell, Harding, the Murrays, Fisher; from Bulmer, Bensley, Strahan, the Whittinghams, and Hansard, to our day, there has been an unbroken and constantly increasing line of clever, practical men, adorning the professions to which they devoted their energies, often realising that fortune which properly directed energies command. In the first half of the century a vast number of splendidly printed books were issued, ornamented in the most lavish manner with beautiful illustrations, engraved on steel or copper plates, and with delicate woodcuts. Book illustration in England may be said now to have reached perfection. When the banker-poet Samuel Rogers wished to bring out an illustrated edition of his works, he employed the two most capable artists of the time, Thomas Stothard and J. M. W. Turner; and they produced an admirable series of designs, which were exquisitely engraved by Finden, Goodall, and Pye. The work was printed by T. Davidson, in two volumes, octavo: the "Italy" in 1830 and the "Poems" in 1834; these two volumes, from the perfect harmony of the typography and illustration and their combined beauty, may be referred to as the perfection of book-making. A very charming series of volumes is found in the "Annuals," "Keepsakes," "Amulets," and similar annual publications, illustrated with beautiful steel plates by the best engravers. The splendidly printed and illustrated bibliographical works of Dr. T. F. Dibdin may also be mentioned. They extend to several volumes, and were printed by Bulmer and his successors Nicoll and T. Bensley, illustrated by engraved plates and woodcuts by F. C. Lewis and others. H. G. Bohn, besides the fine series known as "Bohn's Libraries," numbering over six hundred volumes, in every branch of literature, art, and science, published many finely illustrated books, and as a bookseller had the largest stock of his day. Charles Knight did marvels in popularising literature in his day. William Pickering published a long series of very beautiful books, and in conjunction with Charles Whittingham, printer, of the far-famed Chiswick Press, revived the Aldine or old-faced types; one of the most beautiful of his publications was Sir Harris Nicolas's edition of Walton's "Angler," in two volumes, imperial octavo, with a very fine set of steel plates, designed by Stothard and engraved by Augustus Fox and W. J. Cooke, besides engraved vignettes and representations of fish drawn by Inskipp.

In Germany perhaps the most remarkable achievement of the century is the extraordinary series of volumes of English authors, now (1887) numbering 2,500, issued by Baron Tauchnitz, of Leipzig, which, although eminently popular in their character, are well and tastefully printed. Among the most notable of the printing and publishing houses of Germany, many of them combining the two trades, are J. G. Cotta, dating from 1640; Breitkopf and Härtel, dating from 1719; Justus Perthes, founded 1796; T. O. Weigel, 1797; F. A. Brockhaus, 1805; B. G. Teubner, 1811; W. Drugulin, 1829; J. J. Weber, 1834, etc. Germany has advanced with England and France in fine typography and illustration in their several kinds. The modern school of book illustration in Germany undoubtedly has its origin in the influence given to it by the designs of the artist Adolph Menzel, amongst which a series of two hundred illustrations to the works of Frederick the Great, engraved on wood by the Vogels, Unzelman and Müller, show him to be one of the most powerful and accurate draughtsmen of the century.

To return to France, a new literature arose that was to react against the Greek full of Gallicisms; but the movement, in reversing the ancient state of things, in wishing to replace antiquity by the Middle Ages, old Romans by old French, completely changed the physiognomy of the Book. The engraved vignette and the copper plate of the seventeenth and eighteenth centuries were to lose their supremacy and to give way to etching and wood engraving, also a revival of the Middle Ages.

Fig. 93.—Wood engraving by Clennell after West, for the diploma of the Highland Society.

It is not sufficiently known that wood engraving, after the unfortunate attempts of Papillon in France, was restored in England by Thomas Bewick, who founded a school, of which, at the commencement of our century, Clennell and the brothers Thompson were members. One of the Thompsons went to France about the middle of the Restoration, doubtless with the hope of profiting by his art, and he offered to the Print Department of the National Library the diploma of the Highland Society, a large folio wood block, very adroit and very curiously cut, after the drawing of the celebrated Benjamin West, and copied from Clennell's original block of the same subject. M. Duchesne, then Keeper of the Prints, speaks of this last process as of an apparition: "This print makes apparent the long-neglected and often reappearing art of wood engraving, which, though it could never equal copper engraving, nevertheless merits the attention of amateurs when a capable hand is exercised upon it." It was, we see, a curiosity then, this relief cutting, of which the resurrection was to give an enormous impulse to the Book from the facilities of printing and the economies realised by the possibility of intercalation in periodicals. In fact, metal printing necessitated so much trouble, more for engraving than for the impression. With wood blocks surrounded by type the ordinary press sufficed. The *Magasin Pittoresque*, which was commenced in 1833, and the success of which from the first was very great, was born of these new combinations. Before it the *Messager Boiteux* of Strasbourg and other popular almanacs progressed very well with their illustrations on wood. A kind of firm of engravers, at the head of which were Best and Andrew, undertook the illustrations of the *Magasin Pittoresque*. In a few years progress was immense, other publications came into existence, and a definitive return was made to the vignette in relief. The French illustrated paper preceded our *Illustrated London News* by nine years.

Lavish use was now made of wood engraving, which had thus been suddenly revived in the very midst of the new romantic effervescence, amid a war of books, which, in order to please, had above all to captivate the eye, reacting at once against the spirit and the art of the Restoration. Never before had artists to such an extent taken active part in a purely literary warfare. All the fantastic tendencies of young France were embodied in the lame and halting lines of the time and similar wretched doggerel. Doubtless the leaders of the school did not go quite so far, and their reputation even suffered from such theories; but, as always happens in such cases, the disciples outstripped their masters.

Fig. 94.—Vignette by Devéria for the *Fiancé de la Tombe*.

The brothers Johannot were the first to join in the fray, under the flag of the poets and others of the romantic school, such as Victor Hugo, De Vigny, Paul Lacroix, George Sand, and Devéria, most ruthless of illustrators. The last-named had designed vignettes on wood, of all others, for Baour-Lormian, that is to say for the foe of the new ideas, at once the interpreter of Ossian and the bourgeois bard, full of fire and fury against everything in turn. The *Légendes, Ballades, et Fabliaux*, illustrated by Devéria in 1829, although a sort of compromise with the lovesick swains of mediæval times, did not escape the shafts of ridicule.

In the midst of this movement the Book became democratic; it was printed on sugar-paper for reading-rooms and scullery maids. The generation of romancists diffused its paper-covered works, printing a thousand copies and selling five hundred with great difficulty. Poets publishing five hundred were happy with a sale of two hundred and fifty. Unheard-of titles were then needed to catch the eye, ridiculous and ghastly frontispieces to tickle the fancy of the riffraff. Paul Lacroix called himself the "Bibliophile Jacob," and invented surprising headpieces and foolish designs. And then, as in the fifteenth century, as in the old times, certain signs become popular with the reading public. In the place of the Doctrinals, Complaints, and Disputes, so common in the titles of those epochs, new fancies spring up and have their day. Eccentric devices recommend romantic trash, in which the assassin's dagger, blood, and the horrors of the tomb have replaced the insipid fantasies of the fallen regime. Pétrus Borel, the werewolf, a sort of historic ghoul prowling about the graveyards, enjoyed a monopoly, as it were, of the ghastly titles and contents of this charnel-house literature; it was for his *Champavert*, published in 1833, that Gigoux composed a kind of Bluebeard surrounded by female skeletons, that opened the eyes of publishers to his value as a vignettist.

Although he threw himself soul and body into the romantic movement, the young artist did not alone design subjects called "abracadabrants," following the neologism of the time, any more than the booksellers only published romances. An attempt was made, by publishing them in parts, to still further popularise the old writers at all harmonising with the current taste. The publisher Paulin thus issued the *Gil Blas* of Le Sage, with illustrations in the text by the younger Gigoux, of which the best was hoped. The history of this celebrated enterprise has been written by the artist himself in the curious *Causeries* published recently by him, fifty years after his work on Gil Blas; and this interesting view of an epoch already far distant gives us in a few words the ordinary economy of these popular impressions in parts.

Fig. 95.—Vignette by John Gigoux for *Gil Blas*.

It appears that Paulin, publisher in the Rue de Seine, not being very well off, had associated himself with a man of business named Dubochet, who had before made an enormous fortune with gas. The two represented fifteen thousand to twenty thousand francs, and they ordered a hundred drawings on wood from the young artist. He set to work with precaution, for Dubochet was hard to please, without knowing much about the business, and fined the engravers for the least faults. Gigoux set himself to give his compositions in simple line, without complicated shadows, so as to allow the wood-cutters to preserve a free outline. It was nearly the same thing as the process of the old artists of the fifteenth and sixteenth centuries, of Vostre and Holbein: true engraving in relief. The success of the first sheets was extraordinary; new vignettes were ordered from Gigoux; in place of a hundred they wanted three hundred, then four hundred; then at the end of the work they counted six hundred at least. Money filled the chests of the firm, but when the artist claimed a small share of the benefits, they laughed in his face.

Properly speaking, it was the first serious attempt at illustration by the recovered method of engraving in relief, but it was not the only one. Curmer, the publisher of the Rue Richelieu, prepared a Bible in 1835 and several other volumes, among which were the "Paul and Virginia" and the *Chaumière Indienne* of Bernardin de St. Pierre. He had also collected around him a circle of artists that included Wattier, Devéria, and Meissonier, who was the most perfect and correct of the designers on wood. Meissonier designed very soberly, without effects of light, little scenes admirably cut by an engraver named Lavoignat, a master in the largest sense of the word. Curmer wrote in 1835 in the preface to one of his books, "We hope we have raised a monument to wood engraving. It is easy to judge of the resources presented by this art. We are compelled to have recourse to England to accomplish our work. Peace to willing publishers!"

Fig. 96.—Vignette by Daumier for the *Cholera à Paris*

Curmer acknowledges the importance of English specialists in this new process for vignettes, and the willing publishers were not wanting; they came from all parts. He himself did not stop on the way; he continued his work on a large scale; and Charles Blanc was able to say of him later, as well as of Furne, "He desired to illustrate books for everybody, as the great booksellers of the last century had illustrated their rare editions for a small number of privileged persons." But he did not always confine himself to wood engraving; he also employed etching and lithography. These, requiring separate printing, did not make intercalation with the text any easier than engraving with the burin; but they served to illustrate periodicals, the *Charivari* and *L'Artiste*, as well as some books, where they replaced the engraved plates of the preceding century. At the same time, the latter process was not altogether neglected; about 1840 it was revived, and steel was used in place of copper, as it better resisted repeated impressions. The publisher Furne, while he employed wood engraving, adorned with separate plates on steel his better publications. For him worked Raffet, one of the romanticists enamoured of the Napoleonic epic, which he had popularised, with Charlet and Bellangé, by the pencil, wood, and lithography. Raffet had transferred upon wood, as if in play, the three hundred and fifty-one vignettes of the *Histoire de Napoléon*, by De Norvins, which would to-day suffice for the glory and reputation of many artists. In fact, the analytical and inductive spirit of the artist led him to leave nothing to the chances of inspiration and commonplace of illustration. He laboriously reconstituted, fragment by fragment, the physiognomy of the "old army;" and imbued with the perfect science of detail, he allowed his pencil full play in bold and luminous inventions, where may be seen again, with their peculiar appearance, the heroes of other days, the soldiers of the Rhine and Italy, of Austerlitz and Waterloo.

A truly lively period was that of 1840, a living and unthinking generation. By the side of those great artists of whom we have spoken, and who will be more admired some day, there were the fantasists Traviès and Daumier, who adorned the illustrated journals with innumerable sketches, and Grandville and Gavarni, one caricaturing animals in a celebrated book, *Les Animaux Peints par Eux-mêmes*, which is more than a *chef-d'œvre*; the other coolly studying the vices and faults of his time, with the precision of an anatomist, in *Les Anglais Peints par Eux-mêmes* of Labedollière, in the *Diable à Paris*, without counting a thousand other works which his penetrating imagination produced.

Fig. 97.—Vignette by Gavarni for *Paris Marié*.

Presently photography came, which was to reverse completely the conditions of illustration of the Book by the numerous means of reproduction to which it gave birth. Then wood engraving entered on a new phase, a complete transformation of its ordinary terms, under the influence of Gustave Doré. Little by little it had been attempted to render in relief that which engraved plates only had hitherto done. Black, half-tints, lowered tones, were tried where formerly a simple line, bold and spirited, signified everything. The house of Hachette, founded by one of the normal teachers of the liberal movement, at the beginning of the century, was, together with Lahure, the promoter of relief so inclusive and practical. The numerous periodicals of these publishers spread the taste afar. England, for its part, entered on the road, followed by America and Germany. To-day wood engravings have reached perfection, finesse, and suppleness; but they are not, properly speaking, engravings on wood.

Fig. 98.—Balzac writing his *Contes Drôlatiques*. Vignette by Gustave Doré.

Fig. 99.—Wood block by Bewick, from his "Fables," 1818. The fox and the goat.

We have seen that French publishers were largely indebted to English wood engravers for their blocks. The school that was established by Bewick and his pupils made enormous progress. From the "Fables," published in 1818, we reproduce an illustration as also a specimen from the second volume of the "British Birds." Luke Clennell was one of the most distinguished of Bewick's pupils; and he made some excellent blocks, among them the illustrations to an edition of Rogers's "Poems" (1812), engraved from pen-and-ink drawings by Thomas Stothard. It was Stothard's opinion that wood engraving best reproduced pen-and-ink drawings. Other pupils of Bewick were J. Jackson, John Thompson, who engraved Harvey's beautiful illustrations to Milton and Henderson's "History of Wines," S. Williams, Orrin Smith, Robert Branston, and C. Nesbit. The most prolific and perhaps the most popular book-illustrator of the century in England, was George Cruikshank, who engraved most of his own designs on wood, steel, or with the etching needle; the catalogue of his works by Mr. G. W. Reid, formerly keeper of the Prints in the British Museum, occupies three quarto volumes. The designs of "Phiz," as H. K. Browne called himself, largely contributed to the popularity of the works of Charles Dickens; and the mere mention of Richard Doyle and John Leech will recall the palmy days of *Punch*, although both of these artists did excellent work in book illustration. From the days of the Bewicks to the present wood engraving has formed the most widely used means of illustration in England and the United States. Its adaptability to the printing machine renders it admirably suited to the production of books in large numbers and at low expense. Without it we could not have our *Graphics* and *Illustrated News*, nor the floods of cheap but splendidly illustrated magazines which are appearing on both sides of the Atlantic. True, many of these blocks are due to the "processes" which photography has made available, but they are nevertheless the outcome of wood engraving. We cannot leave this subject without mentioning the admirable "Treatise on Wood Engraving," by W. A. Chatto, with numerous illustrations, published originally by H. G. Bohn in 1839 and since reprinted.

Fig. 100.—Wood block from Bewick's "British Birds." The common duck.

Fig. 101.—Wood engraving by Clennell, after Stothard, for Rogers's Poems, 1812.

In our days the great Paris publishers have returned to the books of the eighteenth century, ornamented with vignettes on copper; many of them purely and simply imitate by photographic processes the pretty editions of Eisen and Moreau, but they do not merit the name which they bear. As to those whose specialty is handsome books with figures by contemporary artists, those who always are in the front, as the Mames, Quantins, Hachettes, Plons, Jouausts, of France; the Longmans, Murrays, Macmillans, Kegan Pauls, Cassells, and Chattos of England; the Harpers, Scribners, Lippincotts, and Houghtons of the United States, they are to us what the ancients of whom we have spoken were to their contemporaries. Now the processes of illustration are without number: wood, metal, heliogravure, phototype, and others. And if the mechanical means, if the heliogravures, have at present the importance claimed, they by no means add to the intrinsic value of wood engravings, but to the rapidity and economy of their manufacture. The Book, the true Book, has nothing to do with all these inventions, and may well confine itself to the burin or the relief block.

But as regards the Book, properly so called, it never was the object of more excessive care or of more unfortunate precipitation. It may be remarked that works least destined to live in the libraries, those thousands of lame pamphlets on questions of small provincial erudition or the cap-and-sword romances, are ordinarily the best and most carefully printed, in opposition to other more important works composed in heads of nails and on worn-out paper. There are in reading-rooms a good number of pamphlets that will not be found in fifty years, and will be worth their weight in banknotes, even if dirty and tattered, on account of their intrinsic value.

CHAPTER VII.

TYPES, IMPRESSION, PAPER, INK.

AFTER this summary, and necessarily very compressed, sketch of the general history of the Book, it will not be without importance to place some technical information before the reader, to explain as clearly as possible the function of the presses, the practical side of typography, from the engraving of the character and the founding of types up to the binding, taking by the way composition, impression, and collation. Many of these operations have been already sketched in the preceding part of our work; we have spoken of engraving of the punch, of impression, of the thousand details that constitute the typographic art, and the knowledge of which is so little diffused. We return to it now, with more method, on the different subjects, and shall try to point out the principal features.

We have seen in our first chapter what patient researches the discovery necessitated for the Mayence printers in the founding of the character in matrix. True, the punch and the matrix had existed from time immemorial for coins and seals. To engrave in relief a punch of material hard enough to strike a resisting metal, and to run into the space obtained by this blow a melted alloy, which took at its extremity the same form as the punch had given, is, in a few words, the whole economy of the process. For the engraving of the punches a sort of burin of tempered steel was used, which scooped out the part intended to remain white in the letter.

From the beginning the printers themselves engraved their own characters. The most ancient, whose constant preoccupation was the imitation of manuscript, copied the Gothic letter of ordinary writing. Soon afterwards, Jenson, the French refugee at Venice, designed a round letter, like that of Sweynheim and Pannartz, the Roman publishers, in 1467; and his type, absolutely perfect, is used to this day.

In France the introducers of the invention in Paris also imitated the Roman, but multiplied abbreviations until they became tedious. We can imagine what the engraving of a character could be where so few letters stood alone, where lines abridged the nasals; the words *pro*, *pre*, figured as in manuscripts; the sign 9 signified *cum* or *con* in Latin or French words, without reckoning a thousand other rigorous usages. This truly perplexing profusion of signs as well as the want of precision and clearness in the letter enables us now to recognise the first Parisian *incunabula*.[6]

[6] See above, figs. 10, 11, 12.

The first English printers used Gothic or black letter. Caxton brought his first fount from Cologne, but that which he made afterwards for himself was of the same character. Wynkyn de Worde, Pynson, and their successors used the same style; and for official publications and Bibles the black letter was used up to the seventeenth century.

Fig. 102.—Type-founder in the middle of the sixteenth century. Engraving by Jost Amman.

But the art of the founder-engraver was destined to specialise itself. There were artisans in this branch, and among them in France, in the fifteenth century, Simon de Collines, who engraved good Roman characters about 1480. Later was Claude Garamond, of Paris, who died about 1561, a pupil of Geoffroy Tory, the most celebrated of all of them; Tory definitely proscribed the Gothic character, of which Vostre and Verard had made constant use. Garamond worked in this way, producing with microscopical precision new letters, among others those of Robert Estienne, the most marvellous and the most distinct. It was he who was charged by Francis I. to form the celebrated royal Greek types. He assisted in getting up the *Champfleury* of Geoffroy Tory.

On his death William Lebé succeeded him, and inherited his punches. Lebé engraved by preference Hebrew characters, of which he made a specialty. His travels to Rome and Venice had given him a singular value in his art; and when he died about the end of the century, he was incontestably the first cutter of Oriental characters in the whole world. Philip II. of Spain had begged him to engrave the letters of the Bible of which Plantin had undertaken the impression, and Francis I. had charged him to make types for the Estiennes.

At the commencement of the seventeenth century we find James Sanlecque, pupil of Lebé, and his son. During this period several women succeeded their husbands as type-founders. In the eighteenth century Philip Grandjean, an artist who was royal printer to Louis XIV., was keeper of the foundry afterwards united, in 1725, to the Royal Printing House; Fournier succeeded the Lebés, then P. S. Fournier the younger, who engraved with great success. In our days we have seen above the Didots themselves working their punches; and one of them, Henri, founded microscopical characters for a La Rochefoucauld about the middle of the nineteenth century.

We have referred to English type-founders of the eighteenth century in Chapter V.

The type, or character used in printing, is a composition of lead and pure antimony, which, melted, form a resisting and at the same time supple mixture. Lead alone would be crushed, and the first printers often suffered in making their experiments. The proportion of the mixture is four of lead to one of antimony.

The matrix is combined in such manner that the *eye*—that is to say, the part of the character intended to produce the impression—and also the shank intended to hold the letter are cast together.

The letters, once founded according to their different forms, are afterwards disposed in boxes with compartments, or "cases." These cases serve to classify the character by letters, italics, capitals, lower case, punctuations, accents, etc.

As we have said, the relation of letters among themselves in the composition of a language is called the "fount." For example, it is certain that the Italian employs the letter *a* more than *b*, the letter *a* appearing in nearly every word; a compositor to compose in this language should therefore have more of *a* than of *b*. The relation between these two letters and all the others is the "fount." In French the proportion of a fount is about 5,000 *a* for 800 *b*, 3,000 *c*, 3,000 *d*, 11,000 *e*, etc. The fount varies with the languages. In English the proportion is 8,500 *a* to 1,600 *b*, 3,000 *c*, 4,400 *d*, etc.

Before 1789 there were in all twenty different "bodies" of letters that bore fantastic names. The "Parisienne" was the smallest size, and the "Grosse Nonpareille" the largest. In the sixteenth century a character called "Civilité" was invented. It sought to imitate fine cursive writing. In the last century this idea was reproduced, and the "Bâtarde Coulée," which did not have great success, was made. In English types, Joseph Moxon in 1669 had eleven sizes; Caslon in 1734 had thirty-eight.

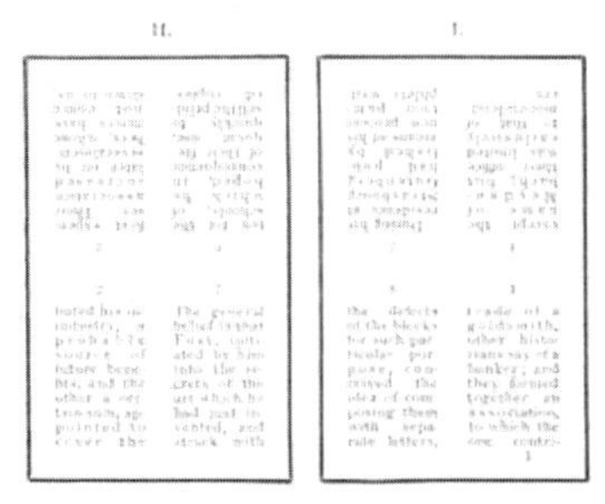

When a printer wishes to compose a work, he first decides in which body he will print it. His choice made, he places in the compositors' "cases"—that is, in the boxes placed before each one of his workmen—the chosen character, with its italics, capitals, signs, etc. Then he gives them the "copy," that is to say the manuscript of the author to be reproduced. The compositors take a "galley" according to the size of the book; and, letter by letter, by running their fingers through the different cases, they place side by side the words laboriously composed, and necessarily presenting their reverse, so that they will show their proper face when printed.

The composition terminated, the process of "imposition" takes place. This is the disposition by pages in an iron chase, in such manner that the sheet of paper shall be printed on both sides, the pages exactly following one another.

It will be seen by the specimen on the preceding page that if the two sheets be brought together, page 2 of II. will fall exactly opposite page 1 of I, page 7 opposite page 8, and so on. Nothing is easier than this combination for folio, quarto, or octavo sizes, but as the smaller sizes are multiplied even to 128mo, tables are necessary to prevent error.

The imposition is completed by building up the composition in a chase by means of pieces of metal called "furniture," which regulate the margins. When the whole is in proper place, it is squeezed up and adjusted by means of sunk reglets. The chase may now be placed under the press without fear of the characters falling out or getting mixed.

A pressman takes a "proof" after having rubbed the relief of the characters with ink, and on this proof are corrected the author's or compositor's faults by indications in the margin by understood signs. By this amended proof the compositor amends his faults one by one: leaves out superfluous characters, puts turned characters straight, spaces or draws closer the lines, etc.

The corrections finished, the time has come to print. In the time of Geoffroy Tory this operation was made as we shall explain; it was the same before and the same after. Two pressmen have tempered with water the tympan, or more elastic part of the carriage, against which will be directed in good time the blow from the type; they have also damped the paper intended for the impression, so that it may retain the greasy ink with which the characters are charged; then the formes are washed before putting them under the press.

In the figure which we reproduce, which dates from about 1530, we see the workshop of Jodocus Badius, of Asch, father-in-law of two celebrated printers, Vascosan and Robert Estienne. The press rolls—that is to say, the formes—have been placed in the "carriage," or movable chase, which, coming forward, receives the sheet of paper and the ink, and returns under the press to receive the blow of the "bar." In the room, lighted by two windows, the compositors work. In front one works at the bar, while his comrade distributes the ink on the "balls." These balls are leather pads, on which the greasy ink, made of lampblack and oil, is spread, to more easily rub the forme after each blow. Ordinarily the inker had two functions: he prepared the ink, distributed it, and kept his eye on the printed sheets to correct faults, blots, and difference of tint. Here the workman is simply occupied by the balls. Printed sheets and prepared paper are on a table by the side of the press. This press is composed of the rolling chase, the tympan, and the "frisket," a smaller tympan, which work against one another. The tympan, we have said above, receives directly the blow. And it was so for nearly four centuries; the mechanical means of our days have a little changed the work, but the principle is always the same.

Fig. 103.—Mark of Jodocus Badius of Asch, representing the interior of a printing office about 1535. Engraving *à la croix de Lorraine*.

Towards the end of the sixteenth century, a press cost about a hundred and twenty-seven crowns, with its diverse utensils, as may be seen in an unpublished piece analysed by Dr. Giraudet, of Tours, in a very interesting pamphlet: *Une Association d'Imprimeurs et de Libraires de Paris Réfugiés à Tours au XVIe Siècle*. The workshop of Jamet Métayer, of Tours, cost a rent of eighty-three crowns—about twenty pounds of current money.

Workmen were then paid by the "day;" and it came to be one of the expressions then so much used in manual labour, corresponding to the sum of the least work of a good workman. M. Ladevèze, printer, thought that the "day" represented the work of about twenty thousand Roman or Cicero letters employed by a compositor.

With us the "day" of compositors and pressmen is differently calculated. The latter have to take a certain number of sheets.

The sheet, composition and press work, cost nearly seven crowns, or nearly two pounds. Jamet Métayer paid twenty crowns for four sheets in Italics; he demanded three months for the work.

The primitive presses were wooden screw presses, and they so remained until the beginning of this century, when Lord Stanhope, a celebrated electrician, author, and politician, perfected them and gave his name to a new machine. His improvement consisted in that the bar was no longer fixed to the vice, but to a cylinder outside. A counter-weight brought back the platen at each blow. Pierre Didot had previously made metal platens. In 1820 the use of the Stanhope press commenced in France.

England had, besides, taken a preponderating place in typographical invention. The printer of the *Times*, John Walter, at the beginning of the nineteenth century, seeking to publish his journal quicker, associated himself with craftsmen who constructed mechanical presses for him. The Didots lost no time, and themselves made improvements.

In 1848, the presses of the *Constitutionnel*, thanks to the application of steam, produced twenty thousand papers an hour. In our time there are machines that print only on one side, as well as double machines, printing both sides at once. The rotary machines, with endless paper, take thirty-five thousand impressions an hour. In the newspaper machines of Marinoni, the great inventor, the paper is unrolled, printed, cut, and folded without leaving the machine, and falls into a place from which it is taken ready for the subscriber. The latest perfection of the printing press is the Walter press and the rotary machine of R. Hoe and Co., of New York, extensively used throughout the world. The elaborate book has little to do with these marvellous processes, although in its turn it largely benefits by the improvement of the printing machine.

Fig. 104.—Paper-making. Workman engaged on the tub with the frame of wires. Engraving by Jost Amman.

It is apart from our purpose to speak at length on the manufacture of paper. It is certain that it was well made before the invention of printing, for most of the accounts of the fifteenth century are written on linen paper, very resisting and well sized. Later on rags were used in this manufacture; and here, in a few words, is how paper was made in the mould, or "hand-made" before the invention of machinery for the purpose:—

The rags, having been thoroughly cleansed, were put into vats, where they were worked up under a beating press until they were reduced to pulp. This pulp was thrown into hot water and stirred until the mixture was uniformly made. Then a mould of fine wire cloth, fixed upon a wooden frame, and having a "deckle" to determine the size of the sheet, was taken; in the middle of this frame was disposed, also in brass wire, a factory mark, intended to appear in white in the sheet of paper, and called the "water mark." This mould was dipped into the vat of pulp and drawn out again. After gently shaking it to and fro in a horizontal position, the fibres of the pulp became so connected as to form one uniform fabric; and the water escaped through the wires. The deckle was then removed from the mould, and the sheet of paper turned off upon a felt, in a pile with many others, a felt intervening between each sheet, and the whole subjected to great pressure, in order to absorb the superfluous water. After being dried and pressed without the felts, the sheets were dipped into a tub of size and again pressed to remove surplus size. This primitive method of paper-making is represented in fig. 104, and the same principle is still in use for the production of hand-made paper. Machinery has effected many improvements and economies in the production of woven paper.

China and Japan have their special paper manufacture. In Japan the material employed is the bark of the *morus papifera sativa.*

Balance used by Jenson, at Venice.

According to their fineness, size, and weight, papers have received different names, proceeding from the water mark.

Faust at Mayence used paper marked with a bull's head. Jenson at Venice used a balance of which the form varied. This latter came from a mill which furnished Vicenza, Perugia, and Rome. Jenson used, besides a crown, a cardinal's hat.

The bull's head underwent transformations, it had stars and roses, and was special to Germany, and it may sometimes be found in Italy.

The wires and bridges served to determine the size of a book. Looking at a folio leaf against the light, the wires will be seen to be horizontal, and the bridges vertical. In quarto they will be reversed, the paper having been folded in four instead of in two. The bridges become horizontal. They return to the vertical in octavo, and so on.

As for ink, it was from the beginning a composition of lampblack and oil of different quality and nature, mixed with resin to obtain a greater and quicker dryness. Ink for engravings was more carefully made. For coloured inks various powders are mixed with the oil and resin, and a title in red and black has to go through the press twice: once for the red and once for the black.

From the above it can be understood that illustrations in relief can easily be introduced into the composition, whether in combination with text or in separate pages. Another question presents itself: Did the old printers employ casting, or did they print directly from the wood block itself? In other words, the block having been cut, did they make with it a mould into which melted metal could be poured to obtain a more resistant relief? The fact is difficult to elucidate. It appears to-day that Simon Vostre, Verard, and others printed relief engravings on metal, but were they cut directly or obtained by casting, as they are now? It cannot be determined yet.

CHAPTER VIII.

BOOKBINDING.

The binding of the first printed books—Ancient German bindings—Binding in the time of Louis XII.—Italian bindings—Aldus—Maioli—Grolier—Francis I.—Henri II. and Diane de Poitiers—Catherine de Medicis—Henri III.—The Eves—The "fanfares"—Louis XIII.—Le Gascon—Florimond Badier—Louis XIV.—Morocco leathers—Cramoisy—The bindings of the time of Louis XIV.—The regency—Pasdeloup—The Deromes—Dubuisson—Thouvenin—Lesné—The nineteenth century—English binders—Roger Payne—Francis Bedford.

LEADING the reader now towards the final perfection of the Book: printing, which had stirred up and reversed so many things, created, so to speak, the art of binding. Previously the binder was simply a workman sewing together the leaves of a manuscript, with no science or device but to clasp the whole together solidly with cord and string. As luxury increased the old binder was no longer thought of. On the wooden boards which closed the Book, jewellers encrusted their wares, lavishing ivory and precious stones to the taste of the amateur or the bookseller. Generally these works covered books of precious miniatures, the *Horæ*, or manuscripts that were deemed worthy of such magnificent clothing, rarely copies without importance. Printing at once disordered the tribe of copyists as well as the binders did jewellers. The demand increasing, rich bindings were soon abandoned, and each bookseller applied himself to the work, or at least covered in his own house books intended for sale. The fashion was not then to expose for sale, as now, unbound books. Purchasers wanted an article easy to handle, and which they were not obliged to return for ulterior embellishment.

So to the public were presented the works laboriously composed by Gutenberg, Schoeffer, and Fust, somewhat after the manner of manuscripts, which they pretended to imitate, with their solid wooden boards covered with pig or calfskin. At the four corners, copper nails, with large heads, prevented rubbing against the shelves of the bookcase, for at that time books were ranged on their sides, and not as they are to-day. We must return to the bibliomaniac of the "Ship of Fools" to get an idea of these depositories; before him may be seen ranged on a desk large folios, with nails on their sides, in the shelves, so defying the dust, in place of being placed upright on their edges, which rendered them liable to spots and stains. (See fig. 23.)

Unhappily the wooden sides had in themselves a germ of destruction, the worm, capable first of reducing the sides to powder and then ravaging the body of the work, the ligatures and cords. Certain preparations destroy the insect, but the precaution often has no effect, and it is thus that the disappearance of volumes formerly so abundant, but almost impossible to find now, may be explained.

Fig. 105.—Bookbinder's shop in the sixteenth century. Engraving by Jost Amman.

From the beginning the operations of the binder were what they still are, except for improvements. They consist in the collation of the sheets of a book, folding them, beating them to bring them together and give them cohesion, and sewing them, first together, then on the cords or strings, which form the five or six bands seen on the backs. Primitively these cords were united to the wooden boards, and over both was placed a resistant skin, on which from relief or metal engravings were struck the most pleasing decorative subjects. Pigskin, white and fine, lent itself, especially among the Germans, to these fine editions; and although they were issued in great number, the wooden boards have not permitted them all to exist in our time.

The most ancient that we are able to cite are German works of the time of Louis XI.; they are very strong and coarse. The cords in them form an enormous and massive projection. The inside of the board was often without lining of paper or stuff. In the case of fine editions a sombre velvet was sometimes used, such as Verard used to bind the books of the father of Francis I., as we have before said.

Art did not enter into these works of preservation until about the end of the fifteenth century, with arms and emblems. At the beginning of the sixteenth century, some bindings were ornamented for Louis XII. and the Queen, Anne de Bretagne; but not more than five or six specimens remain. They are of coarse aspect. The workman who tooled the binding here reproduced from the curious example of M. Dutuit, of Rouen, has thrown his subjects one upon another. Arms, porcupines, ermines, are treated so as to be confusing, and form a medley that is not pleasing. In recalling the delightful borders of Vostre and Pigouchet, contemporaries of this mediocre work, it is astonishing to see the degree of inferiority reached by a profession that should be inspired by graceful subjects of decoration.

Fig. 106.—Binding for Louis XII. Collection of M. Dutuit, of Rouen.

It happened that France again found in Italy masters capable of revealing secrets of composition and arrangement to enable her to strike out a new road. The Italian wars would not have had these artistic results if it had not been for the enormous sums that they swallowed up. The curious part of the enterprise was that a war treasurer, a financier, employed by the French kings in these expeditions, through his relations of taste and friendship with the Alduses of Venice, brought to France the love of sumptuous bindings, of editions superbly clothed. He was named Jean Grolier, that bibliophile of the sixteenth century, who was, above all others, even King Francis, the first to appreciate the art of binding. It is not too much to say art, for if better had not been done before, it may safely be said that nothing better has been done since; and the books of Grolier remain as the most perfect and most admirable types of this kind of decoration.

Born of an Italian family established at Lyons, where most of his relatives did a great business, Jean Grolier had the good fortune to succeed his father, Stephen Grolier, treasurer of the Duke of Milan. He became in his turn Minister of Finances, and was called to accompany the kings in their expeditions in Italy. The situation of the treasurers during these campaigns was important; they handled the pence levied with great trouble in the cities of France "for making war." Many abused their trust, and were punished, and among others the Lallemants, whom documents show us to have been in connection with Grolier, and who suffered, with Semblançay, the most terrible trials of the time.

Italian art gave then a free course in the decoration of books. Of the interior we have spoken in our first chapters on the wood engravings; for the exterior, the cover of the volume, foliage, golden flowers worked with a hot iron, and polychromatic compartments obtained by coloured pastes were multiplied. Thus was produced on the outside that which it was not sought to obtain on the inside, the variation of tints so select among the Italians, and so forsaken since the invention of printing. In the midst of these literary men was a lover of books and fine connoisseur who, not content with choosing the best editions, such as those of Ferrara, Venice, and Basle, bound them superbly, with compartments of admirable tone, and had his name and device inscribed on the sides in the fashion of the time. He was named Thomas Maioli, and following the custom of the amateurs of the time, he offered the enjoyment of his library to his friends. "Tho. Maioli et amicorum," he inscribed, as did later Grolier, as also did others, but he somewhat modified the enthusiasm of his friendship by a sceptical device, "Ingratis servire nephas," which might very well be the cry of the owner of books betrayed by his borrowers.

Maioli did not alone use these devices; he had also a macaronic phrase of which the sense is not very clear: "Inimici mei mea michi, non me michi." He also sometimes used his monogram, which was composed of all the letters of his name.

The relations of Grolier with this unknown and mysterious bibliophile, whose name is not always found outside his volumes, are not doubtful. Brunet possessed a volume that had belonged to Maioli and had passed through the hands of Grolier. What better proof could be wished of the communion of ideas and tastes between the two collectors?

But these amateurs were not alone. Beside them were princes and great lords, lay and ecclesiastic. From the commencement of the sixteenth century bookbinding had received an enormous impulse from the tastes and the predilections for these lofty fancies. And it cannot be ascribed to the simple skill of the workmen experimenting in that line. In the century that saw Italian artists occupied in making designs for mounted plates and painting beautiful ladies, the courtesans of Venice could not be alarmed at finding them painting models for bindings, with compartments of varied tone and style. Maioli affected white on a dark background, that is to say on a background of dark leather. He made scrolls of foliage in white or clear paste with a very happy effect.

This was the time when Grolier travelled in Italy, in the suite of the French, and when he began his collections. He had adopted as his heraldic emblem the gooseberry bush, which in French came very near to his name —*groseillier*; and his motto was "Nec herba nec arbor" ("Neither tree nor herb"), explicative of the moderation of his wealth. He was soon in connection with the Alduses, and through them with the principal learned men and binders of the time, for it was not in the offices of the Manutiuses that could be found workmen, like those of the Chamber of Accounts in France, obliged to swear that they did not know how to read. The master was not hindered by details of difference of language, and it followed that his workmen understood Greek and Latin, for he often gave them instruction in those languages. How far off these erudite and conscientious workmen appear to-day!

Following the fashion, Grolier put his name on the upper side of his books —"Jo. Grolierii et amicorum"—in gold letters, and on the other side a pious motto, the sense of which was a hope often uttered by the financiers of the sixteenth century, imprisoned and hung every instant: "Portio mea, Domine, sit in terra viventium." Generally all the Grolier books which came from the Alduses have the name on the upper side and the motto on the other side; the title was placed above the name, and often disposed in rows. Some large volumes had the cover ornamented with an architectural design, like the Jamblichus of the Libri collection, which had on the front the façade of a temple, with the title in rows on the door. This volume was printed by Aldus in 1516, and probably decorated by him for the account of the great French amateur.

Jean Grolier is said to have himself designed some of the subjects of his ornaments, and their perfection indicates an active and enlightened supervision. On his return to France, where he had a house near the Porte de Bucy, he was put in relation with Geoffroy Tory, the artist best fitted to understand him, and who was at once painter, engraver, printer, and binder. It was there that, in the leisure of his financial functions, between two projects of revictualling the forts of Outre Seine and Yonne, Grolier invented combinations, sought interlacings, and laid out foliage. Tory himself teaches us these works in combination. He invented antique letters for Grolier, he tells us in his *Champfleury*. It was for him, too, that he interwove so finely his compartments for binding, and that he reproduced the delightful ornaments of his books of hours in golden scrolls.

As we have said, Grolier placed his titles on the sides of his books on account of the arrangement of the works on the shelves of the library where they were laid. For this reason also the back was neglected, and no ornament used upon it; thick and heavy with its projecting bands, without decoration between the bands, this part of the bound volume was a kind of waste in a splendidly cultivated garden. The profusion of books brought about a revolution. There was no longer room to place on their sides the innumerable books that were produced; they were then placed on their edges, as now, and the back also was decorated. For this the bands were made to disappear, and replaced by decorative subjects in compartments like the sides. Then with Grolier the bands reappeared, and the title was placed between them, as it still is.

The books of Grolier have been divided, according to their production, in four or five principal classes, in which they may always be placed. First were the works ornamented in compartments, gilt, with scrolls in full gold; then the same with the scrolls *azurés*, that is to say equally gilt, but having parallel lines like the *azure* of heraldry. Following comes the school of Geoffroy Tory, with gilt compartments in the style of the great French decorator; last the polychromatic bindings, in which, by the aid of colour or mastic, the alternating tones are mixed. Grolier also had some mosaic bindings, composed of little pieces of leather connected by incrustation or paste, pure Italian bindings; but these were not numerous, especially if compared with those conceived in the manner of Geoffroy Tory.

One of these latter works is here reproduced from one of the beautiful books in the collection of M. Dutuit. This copy has the back flat, and the interlacings of the decoration are most complicated and clever.

Grolier got his Levant moroccos through the dealers of Venice to be sure of the material he employed.

Fig. 107.—Binding for Grolier in the collection of M. Dutuit.

Born in 1479, the Treasurer-general of Outre Seine lived until 1565. In 1563 an original manuscript shows him much occupied with finance at over eighty-four years of age; but his passion for bindings had cooled down, for few books signed with his name are found the manufacture of which could descend to the son of Henri II. After great trials, after having seen Semblançay suffer at Montfaucon, John Lallemand beheaded, and himself having come nearly to losing life and fortune at one blow, Grolier passed away quietly in his house, having collected most of the fine books of the time and many curious medals. Christopher de Thou, his friend and *confrère* in the love of books, had saved his reputation before the Parliament of Paris. After his death his library was transported to the Hotel de Vic, and from there dispersed in 1675, a hundred years after.

Thus from Italian art came French binding, still remaining original. The kings did not fail to follow the movement, and even to anticipate it, thanks to the means at their disposal. We have seen Francis I. at work with the energy of an artisan at least; but Geoffroy Tory was his principal inspirer, and who knows but that he was the chief operative for the prince, as for the great financier?

Fig. 108.—Binding for Francis I., with the arms of France and the salamander.

Fig. 109.—Mark of Guyot Marchant, printer and bookbinder. He published the *Danse Macabre* of 1485.

We have said that Louis XII. knew nothing of fine bindings. During his travels in Italy he had received presentation copies of magnificently covered books, and among others that of *Faustus Andrelinus*, that was bound in calf in honour of the King. He, who was so little expert in fine arts, purchased the entire library of the Sire de la Gruthuse, and substituted his own emblems for those of the high and mighty lord. Francis I., with innate sentiment for masterpieces and the powerful protection he had given them, did not allow the experiments of Grolier to pass unnoticed. The King did not desire to be behind the treasurer, and the workmen were put to the task. He adopted the salamander, which emblem he used on his castles and furniture and the liveries of his people; he lavished it also on the sides of his books. On the side the "F" is often seen crowned, then the emblem of France and the collar of St. Michael. In the binding of which a facsimile is here given, Geoffroy Tory has singularly inspired the gilder, if he did not himself make the design. For it must not be thought that this work is done at a single blow by means of an engraved plate or a block. On the contrary, every line is impressed by the hot tool that the workman applies by hand to the gold laid on in advance, making it, so to speak, enter into the skin or morocco. There is the art; blocks serve only for commercial bindings, quickly impressed and intended for ordinary purchasers.

Fig. 110.—Binding for Henri II., with the "H" and crescents.

Under the reign of Francis I. the binders were the booksellers, as Verard and Vostre were. The King was ordinarily served by a publisher named Pierre Roffet, and he frequently figures in accounts that have been preserved. Roffet not only bound, but it appears that he rebound books to patterns which the King desired. Philip Lenoir and Guyot Marchant were also royal workmen. The latter, whose mark is here reproduced, frequently added to it the saints Crispin and Crispinian, patrons of the leather-dressers, who prepared the leather for the binder.

Fig. 111.—Binding for Henri II. (Mazarine Library)

The discoveries of Grolier did not allow the binders much time to be idle. Thousands of volumes were then destroyed to make the boards for sides. From this many discoveries are made in our days by pulling to pieces sixteenth century work, unknown playing cards, and early printed works. To mention only one example, twenty leaves of the "Perspective" of Viator were discovered in the National Library of Paris. The board thus formed was covered indifferently with sheepskin, parchment, calf, morocco, or goatskin; the books were sewn on raised or sunk bands, according to the owner's taste; the edges were gilt, sometimes gauffered, and designs often impressed upon them to match those of the sides. In large folios wooden boards were still used, more solid, and protected from rubbing by nails in relief. But the inside of the cover was as yet only covered with paper. Leather linings were very uncommon.

The reign of Henri II. increased yet more the importance of bindings; it was the time when Grolier collected, and clever artists came from all parts. Geoffroy Tory had given the best models for letters and interlacings. The Queen, Catherine, derived from her parents the taste for decoration in gold and colours, and patronised the artists called by her from the court of Florence; and the favourite, Diane de Poitiers, Duchess of Valentinois, rivalled her in luxury and expenditure. Henri II. in the decoration of his castles, as well as his books, introduced equivocal emblems, of which the signification may be doubtful, but those of his mistress may be recognised, not those of the legitimate Queen. He interlaced two reversed "D's" by an "H," in the form shown in the border on the preceding page. Strictly speaking, we ought to see there two "C's" back to back; but as we find the "D" on all the bindings displaying the arms of Diana, there can be no doubt, and Queen Catherine doubted less than anybody. Other emblems of Diana are to be found in the arcs and crescents that are plentifully displayed. The library of Diana was large, owing to the King not hesitating to take valuable books from the public collections for her. Two centuries after her death it was dispersed, and the greater part of the books belonging to the national collections were restored on the deaths of those who then purchased them. Hence the largest number of the bindings of Henri II. and Diana of Poitiers will be found in the National Library of Paris.

Fig. 112.—Italian binding for Catherine de Medicis, with the initials "C. C."

Queen Catherine also had special patterns with a monogram identical with the double "D" mentioned above, but the branches of the "C" were a little longer than the branches of the "H;" she also used a "K" on the sides of her books. The specimen which we reproduce is a purely Italian work.

From kings and queens the fashion passed to the great lords, it having come to the kings and queens from a private individual. The Constable Anne de Montmorency adorned his bindings with a cross and spread eagle. Among the amateurs of binding of the sixteenth, seventeenth, and eighteenth centuries using distinctive marks, we may mention Philip Desportes, the poet, who used two Φ enlaced, as did also Superintendent Fouquet in the seventeenth century. The brothers Dupuy adopted the double Δ, arranged as a star. Colbert had a curled snake (*coluber* for Colbert!), the Gondis two masses of arms, Madame de Pompadour three towers, etc. Fouquet beside the Φ used a squirrel on some of his bindings.

In Germany, Count Mansfeldt adopted the ornamental style with arms, of which a specimen is here given; and Marc Laurin de Watervliet also decorated and dedicated his books to his friends, using the motto "Virtus in arduo." Among the lords of the French courts who favoured polychromatic ornament and bold compositions were the young Valois, Louis de Sainte Maure, Marquis of Nesle, and Henri de Guise, called "Le balafré."

Fig. 113.—Binding with the arms of Mansfeldt, with *azure* scroll work, from the Didot collection.

Charles IX. had his emblems and devices, the double "C" crowned the legend "Pietate et justitia," but his brother, Henri III., loved the decoration of books more than he did. The passion of the King for miniatures which he cut out of books is known; this passion for golden things he repeated on bindings, for which he chose special designs. Henri III. was an amateur of dances of death; he visited cemeteries, attended funerals, and took a death's-head for his emblem. This emblem was not his invention; long before him Marot had addressed an epigram to a lady in which he brought love and death into close conjunction. However that may be, the King chose skeletons and penitents' tears to ornament his books. He also tolerated diamonds, although he absolutely prohibited them in the clothing of ladies or fixed the number *pro rata* with the rank of the authorised person. There was in this prince a singular mixture of taste and artistic acuteness by the side of a mania or hallucination which was reflected on the most intimate objects of his apparel or of his furniture. Thus if we find, at the end of the sixteenth century, a death's-head on the sides or the back of a volume, the binding is of the period of Henri III.

Fig. 114.—Sixteenth century binding, called *à la fanfare*. In the Dutuit collection.

The binders of his time are known by the mention that is made of them in the royal accounts; the Eves were the most celebrated among all of them. Nicholas Eve was charged with the binding of the Statutes of the Order of St. Esprit, with which the King gratified his friends. Mention of this work is found in the Clairambault manuscripts, where we read, "To Nicholas Eve, washer and binder of books and bookseller to the King, forty-seven and a half escus for washing, gilding, and squaring the edges of forty-two books of statutes and ordinances of the Order, bound and covered with orange Levant morocco, enriched on one side with the arms of the King, fully gilt, and on the other of France and Poland, with monograms at the four corners, and the rest flames, with orange and blue ribbons," etc.

Louise de Lorraine, wife of Henri III., counted for little in the life of her husband; nevertheless she had a certain number of books decorated with their united escutcheons.

The bindings attributed to Eve were decorated all over the sides and back with interlacing patterns of geometrical character, the spaces between the parallel lines and in the middle of the figures left at first quite blank, but afterwards filled in with palm branches and wreaths of foliage; to these delicate and elaborate yet brilliant toolings have been given the name of bindings *à la fanfare*. This designation requires explanation, and is a good example of the grotesque style adopted by modern amateurs in their appellations.

The fine work of that time prepared for the coming in the seventeenth century—about 1620—of the works of Le Gascon, or at least for the artist with whom in our days are connected the works of the reign of Louis XIII. Under Henri IV. the fleur-de-lys occupied most of the covers of the royal books, from vellum to Levant morocco; works in this class had nothing very remarkable. The first years of Louis XIII. revealed a new process, inspired by the Eves. Le Gascon embroidered delightfully on the fanfare ornaments; showing the fibres of the leaves, he made a new kind of ornament, consisting of minute gold dots elaborated into lines and curves of singular brilliancy and elegance. Of this style, called *pointillé*, we give a specimen from the collection of M. Dutuit. The fashion had arrived all at once; lace, banished from clothing by severe edicts, found a refuge on the covering of books.

Fig. 115.—Le Gascon binding.

The times were hard then for binders; they were constrained to live in the university and to employ only its workmen. A binder was never his own gilder; he employed the *gaufreurs* of shoe-leather, more expert and bolder, to gild his leather. Among these artisans was one named Pigorreau, whom the edict found living in the midst of publishers and working for them; he was compelled to choose either to remain bootmaker or become bookseller; he chose the latter, against the syndics of the trade, against every one, and he made enemies for himself. He revenged himself by turning the masters into ridicule in a placard.

Le Gascon was probably the assumed name of an artist in this style. The *Guirlande de Julie*, worked by him for Mademoiselle de Rambouillet, gave him great honour in the special circle of this little literary court. It was the fashion then for poor authors to put a fine covering on their works and to offer them to the great for their own profit. Tallement des Reaux notably signalises the poet Laserre, who displayed his luxury in irreproachable bindings. And then the farmers of the revenue, successors of Grolier in financial trusts, formed libraries for pure fashion, never opening the volumes covered for them in sumptuous attire. If we may believe Sauval, author of the *Antiquités de Paris*, they went further, and on covers without books inscribed imaginary titles and fantastic squibs to mislead their visitors. The bookcase being carefully closed, it was difficult to discover the imposition. Sauval writes, "In place of books, they are content with covers of Levant morocco, on the backs of which, in gold letters, are inscribed the names of the most celebrated authors. A binder of the university assured me that not long since he and his *confrères* had made them for a single financier to the amount of 10,000 crowns!"

Fig. 116.—Le Gascon binding for Cardinal Mazarin.

The works of Le Gascon will be found more among great personages than with the so-called collectors, which gives value to their grace and charm. The King's brother Gaston possessed them, then Mazarin, an example from whose library is here reproduced. On this binding Le Gascon worked gilt compartments and elaborate arabesques; in the middle of the sides are the arms of the Cardinal and his pretentious device: "Arma Julii ornant Franciam!"—"The arms of Jules the ornament of France!" In spite of the profusion of subjects, nothing could better please the eye or indicate a man of taste.

But if Le Gascon be a legendary personage, he had an imitator or rival, very near to him, named Florimond Badier, whose works had at least the advantage of being signed. At the bottom of the inside cover of an inlaid morocco binding in the National Library at Paris is the inscription "Florimond Badier fec., inv." The analogy between this work and those known as Le Gascon's is palpable; inside and outside, the cover is stippled with small tools (*au petit fer*) in the same manner. Florimond Badier was not appointed bookseller until 1645, and so could not have composed earlier bindings attributed to Le Gascon, but this resemblance of style evidences the existence of a Parisian school, the adepts of which copied one another, as they do nowadays.

The work was soon simplified; pallets and wheel-shaped tools were invented to produce that which was improperly called *dentelle*; this mechanical work was done by a wheel-shaped tool, previously heated, on gold in sized leaves, on which it impressed its projections.

With Louis XIV. the passion for gilding increased. Charming festoons were designed, but they were soon abused, and inundated the libraries. On the sides were seen rising suns, arms, and golden garlands. Cramoisy directed the royal bindings, the King having devoted large sums to the purchase of Levant leathers. In 1666 the Director of Works ordered red moroccos; in 1667 he received twenty-two dozen skins, amounting, with the expenses of transport, to 1,020 livres tournois. Successive supplies were made, and were used for the royal library, sixty-nine dozen in 1667, forty-six dozen in 1668, and three hundred and thirty-three dozen in 1670, costing the King more than 12,000 livres. On these admirably dressed skins, which, in spite of incessant use, still remain now as in their first days, the King caused to be applied, according to the size, tools of borders, having in the middle the arms of France, with the collar of St. Esprit.

Among the binders mentioned in the very useful work of M. J. J. Guiffrey on the expenditure of Louis XIV., we find Gilles Dubois, who died before 1670; Levasseur, binder of Huet, Bishop of Avranches; La Tour, Mérins or Mérius, who died before 1676; and also Ruette, the reputed inventor of marbled paper for fly-leaves of books: to him the bindings of the Chancellor de Séguier, with their ornament of the golden fleece, and of Madame de Séguier, are attributed. It was probably these men who decorated the books of the brothers Dupuy, Fouquet, and Colbert, marvellous works of solidity, if not always of elegance, which have resisted all assaults. Unhappily, in many instances the mechanical *dentelle* overburdened the work, and gave it a commonplace regularity. In the Condé, Colbert, and perhaps even Madame de Longueville's collections, there are many specimens of this kind with two or three filleted borders.

We have come to an epoch when the difficulties resulting from confusion between the booksellers' and binders' trades began to be understood. The revocation of the Edict of Nantes had implicitly prepared a crowd of measures and rules in all branches of national industry. It was a good occasion to prevent the artisans of binding unduly parading themselves as booksellers and selling merchandise of which they understood nothing; Louis XIV. interfered, and separated the two communities. The binders then became the *relieurs-doreurs* of books; they had their own organisation, but remained subject to the university; the heads of the fraternity were called the "guards." The principal arrangements of the regulation of 1749 were: the members of the corporation had the sole right to bind books, from the elegant volume to registers of blank paper. Five years of apprenticeship and three of companionship were necessary to obtain the brevet of freedom and to hold a shop. Moreover, it was indispensable to read and write. One regulation ordained that the workman should be "able to bind and ornament ordinary books or others, to render them perfect and entire, to sew the sheets at most two together with thread and real bands, with joints of parchment, and not paper, and in case of infraction the said books were to be remade at the expense of the offender, who was besides condemned to a penalty of thirty livres for each volume." Their establishment was confined to the quarter from the Rue St. André des Arts to the Place Maubert; they regulated the sale of calfskin and of tools; in a word, they were surrounded by precautions by which the production remained always under the supervision of the masters and completely satisfied the client. This calculating policy was, in fact, a close imitation of the royal ordinance of 1686.

Fig. 117.—Mosaic binding of the eighteenth century for the *Spaccio de la Bestia Trionfante*.

The mosaic bindings used from the end of the reign of Louis XIV. were an application of pared leathers of colours different from the background, pasted on to the side. The binders of the regency composed a great number, attributed now to Pasdeloup, as all the crayons of the sixteenth century are called Clouets, and all the panels on wood Holbeins. It is not that there was great originality in these works, or a particular art; more often the workman did no more than transcribe Le Gascon or Eve or the older binders, and accommodated the processes of these artists to the fashion of his time. In this style we may cite the *Spaccio de la Bestia Trionfante*, printed at Paris 1584, for which the binder designed a cover of doubtful taste and, above all, an undeniable want of proportion. The tendency was then to flowers occupying three-fourths of the page, to compartments too large, to open pomegranates, like the *Spaccio* here reproduced. If Pasdeloup had discovered these mediocre combinations, he could not be proclaimed the regenerator of a fallen art. The bastard style of these works may be compared to their mosaics, constructed of pieces; it is a little of everything, and together it is nothing. However, in the midst of the quantity of mediocre things, some pleasing decoration is from time to time met with; the design of a volume with the arms of the Regent and his wife, Mademoiselle de Blois, wants neither elegance nor taste; without being perfection, it has better proportion and balance.

Fig. 118.—Mosaic binding of the eighteenth century, with the arms of the Regent. M. Morgand's collection.

We should, however, hesitate to give names to all these works. Besides Pasdeloup, there were the Deromes, abandoning a little the mosaics, devising flowers and *dentelles* in combination, and no longer the simple products of the fillet. They formed a dynasty; and if the Pasdeloups were at least twelve, there were fourteen Deromes all booksellers and binders from the reign of Louis XIV. The most celebrated was James Anthony, who died in 1761.

Peter Paul Dubuisson was not only a binder; he was a designer. He invented heraldic ornaments, and composed models of gilding tools, in which his contemporaries emulated him. He was intimate with the delicate vignettist Eisen, and the counsels of an artist of this value could not but be useful to him. It is an extraordinary thing that in this world of celebrated printers, amateur financiers, and notable painters and engravers, not a single man can be met to give a real impulse to the art of which we speak, and to prevent the dull continuance of experiments on the whole so poor. Doubtless the *dentelles* of Derome had a certain air of gaiety, to which the books of the eighteenth century accommodated themselves perfectly; the tools of Dubuisson produce most pleasing designs; but the old, the great binders, had altogether disappeared.

Besides, Derome massacred without pity the rarest works. He loved edges very regularly cut, and he did not fail to hew down margins opposed to his taste. He sawed books as well; that is to say, in place of sewing the sheets on to projecting bands, he made a groove in the back, in which the cord was embedded. The books have no resistance.

To these celebrated names of French binders of the eighteenth century we may add Le Monnier, who worked for the Orleans princes; Tessier, his successor; Laferté, who decorated the small volumes of the Duc de la Vallière as Chamot covered the large ones; in 1766 Chamot was royal binder. There was also Pierre Engerrand, then Biziaux, an original, who worked for Madame de Pompadour and Beaumarchais. Boyet, or Boyer, worked (1670-80) in the style of Le Gascon, with the same minute tooling, but simpler in character. Duseuil put very elaborate and delicate tooling on his covers from about 1710 to 1720.

The Revolution effaced many of the fine works which displayed the symbols "of a royalty justly detested," and Mercier wrote certain wicked little poems against binding. Lesné was the poet of bookbinding, and he invented the process of plain calf without boards. Certainly from Grolier to Lesné there were numerous changes, so numerous that, in spite of the nude calf, it may be said that the art was nearly dead. In our days it has a little recovered. Amateurs have found new names, and often artists, to patronise: Trautz-Bauzonnet, Capé, Duru, Lortic, Marius Michel, in France; Bedford, Rivière, Zaehnsdorf, Pratt, in England; Matthews, Bradstreet, Smith, in the United States; and many others. Unhappily, fortune does not permit every one to furnish his library luxuriously; the true connoisseur searches rather for Groliers, Eves, and Le Gascons, than concerns himself about modern workmanship. Whatever may be its value, it is only fit to clothe the works of the time. A book published by Lemerre and bound by Petit is in true character, but a fifteenth or sixteenth century book passed under the hands of Trautz-Bauzonnet himself will be very much like an ancient enamel in a modern frame newly gilt.

Bookbinding in England has, with very few exceptions, never attained the artistic excellence reached in France. From the earliest times to the present day servile imitations of foreign work only are seen. The one purely original English binder is Roger Payne, who from about 1770 worked for thirty or forty years in London, performing with his own hands every stage of the work, even to cutting his own tools. The result was good, solid work, with perfectly original and often very beautiful decoration, appropriate to the character of the work itself. His favourite style was drooping lines of leaf ornaments in the borders and geometrical patterns in small tools. After him came Charles Lewis, who was an artist in the true sense of the word, and, coming down to our own time, Francis Bedford, who, never pretending to originality, copied the best designs of the old French and Italian binders. His full calf books, with handsomely tooled backs, are models of solidity and taste; and his decorations on the sides of morocco-bound books are always in good taste, and often of great elegance. The binders of the present day, perhaps for lack of patronage, seem to have abandoned originality; and although much excellent work is done, it is no more than a copy of the Eves, Le Gascon, Derome, and the older artists.

Parallel with the luxurious bindings with which we have been exclusively occupied, there has always been the commercial work, prepared in advance. Liturgical works, above all, are sold in this form. Books in the Grolier style or other grand personages were worked from a pattern engraved in relief, leaving nothing to the caprice of the artist, by being applied to the side by a press. This process is termed blocking. Germany made use of this process principally; also Vostre, Verard, and Tory employed the same means. Even the interlacings and the capricious arabesques of Grolier were imitated by means of a fixed plate, parts of which were finished by hand to make it appear a complete work of imagination and handicraft.

CHAPTER IX.

LIBRARIES.

RT, science, and literature took refuge in convents before the invention of Printing, and libraries did not count many books. According to daily wants, the monastery scribes copied the treatises lent by neighbouring houses, and the collection was thus painfully made during many centuries. Two or three hundred works constituted ordinary collections; the powerful abbeys found in their staff the means of enriching their libraries, as we have said, but they were the privileged ones.

Excepting kings and some princes, few people possessed a library. The great expense of transcription, the want of facility for procuring originals, and the enormous price of manuscripts left no hope to bibliophiles of moderate fortune. Typography, on the contrary, having multiplied books and put at relatively modest prices reproductions formerly inaccessible, private collections commenced. We have had occasion to speak before of Grolier and Maioli; they were the most illustrious, but not the only ones.

At first a public library was an unknown thing. The richest and the most easily got together, that of the King of France, was private. Since John the Good in France the acquisitions were numerous, and Gutenberg's invention contributed to augment the stock of volumes everywhere. Charles VIII. and Louis XII. found or took in their expeditions in Italy, and were able to add to the original nucleus, many rare editions, especially from the Sforzas at Pavia, who had marvels without number. Brought together at Blois, under the care of John de Labarre, the royal library did not yet occupy a very large space, in spite of its increase. Under Charles V. the number of books was about a thousand; about 1500 or 1510 they were nearly doubled, and the printed books did not number more than two hundred.

So restricted, the royal library travelled with the other treasures of the Crown; Francis I. transported it from Blois to Fontainebleau, and even parts of it to the Italian wars, as related above. In its new quarters the royal collection, in spite of the successive accessions of the books of John d'Angoulême, grandfather of the King, and of those of the dukes of Orleans, counted but 1,781 manuscripts and a hundred and nine printed books on the shelves. The King, ambitious in literature no less than in arts, nominated an illustrious *savant*, Guillaume Budé, to the office of master of his library; and this qualification was maintained by his successors until the fall of the royal power.

With Budé commenced the system of continuous acquisitions. The treasury was liberally opened to vendors of rarities. At this time the books, placed upon their sides, one upon another, gave no idea of a modern library, with its volumes ranged on end, having their titles between the bands of the back. In speaking of Grolier, we remarked that the sides of a binding alone had importance on account of their place on the shelves; it was the same with Francis I.

Under Henri II. the Fontainebleau collection was somewhat pillaged for Diana of Poitiers, but, as a corrective for this dilapidation, the King adopted a measure, since preserved, which substituted for acquisitions a regular and uninterrupted supply; this was the contribution by publishers to the library of one bound copy on vellum of all the works printed under privilege. The ordinance was made in 1556; the successors of Henri II. had only this means of increasing the number of their volumes, with the exception that Charles IX. expended a large sum in the purchase of Grolier's collection of medals.

Such was the working of the royal library for about a half-century, but the idea of making it public had not come. Diffused as was then the passion for books, it had not yet been democratised to the point of being understood by the people. Amateurs and lovers of reading formed special collections in their houses, at times rivalling that of the King. Then the fashion was no more to lay the books on their sides, but they were now ranged to allow room for new acquisitions. Henri IV., who had not his great-uncle's predilection for Fontainebleau, commanded the removal to Paris of the books buried in the castle. He added to them those of Catherine de Medicis coming from Marshal Strozzi; and as the college of Clermont had become vacant by the dispersion of the Jesuits, he lodged the library in 1599 in one of the rooms of that establishment, under the care of James Augustus de Thou, master of the library.

We now see the royal collection brought to Paris, which it has never quitted; but before its definitive installation, before it was made public, it passed through a century, during which additions were made, purchases increased, and the number of manuscripts and printed books augmented in enormous proportions. Henri IV. desired to place it near the court, to avoid pillage and to have the chief librarian near to him. The return of the Jesuits in 1604 upset the first establishment a little; the college of Clermont was evacuated; the books were transported to the Cordeliers and distributed in rooms on the ground and first floors, whence the names of upper and lower libraries. There was a mass of volumes very little used, for the public did not enjoy them, and the King held them as his own; but the time was near when the collection was to take a very serious step under the influence of the brothers Dupuy in 1645, and afterwards of Jerome Bignon. Always shut up in the incommodious chambers of the Cordeliers, the library contained 5,259 volumes, manuscript and printed, perhaps less than some private libraries; after the Dupuys it had at least 10,329 printed books.

Mazarin was the first to comprehend the natural use of collections of books: publicity. His private library, placed before 1651 in his magnificent house in the Rue Richelieu, where later was definitively lodged the royal library, was opened to readers every Tuesday, from eight to eleven and two to five. Dispersed in 1651, at the fall of the Cardinal, it was later reconstituted, and in less than ten years afterwards the former minister was able to open it in its new quarters, the College of the Four Nations, where it is still.

While the Mazarin library was administering liberally to the wants of the public, that of the King remained closely shut up in the rooms of the Cordeliers. Colbert, influenced by this state of things, offered two houses in the Rue Vivienne to the King, where the books could find a more convenient lodging, and allow room for increase. The removal was made in 1666. The royal collection for fifty-five years was lodged only a few steps from its final resting-place, the Hotel de Nevers. So was called at the end of the seventeenth century the splendid mansion of Mazarin, situated near the Porte de Richelieu, in the street of the same name, whence his books had been previously torn and sold to all the dealers. Divided into two parts at the death of the Cardinal in 1661, the palace fell, one part to the Duc de Mazarin, the other to the Duc de Nevers, his nephews. At first the King dreamed, under the advice of Louvais, of acquiring the land in the neighbourhood of the Rue Vivienne and of elevating a monument for his library, for the thought of putting the Hotel de Nevers to this use had not then occurred to him; but the Duc de Mazarin having alienated his part of the palace in favour of the Company of the Indies, Abbé Bignon, then royal librarian, perceived the part he could play from that fact.

Thanks to the administration of Colbert and the liberalities of the King, the collection had been augmented threefold. At the time of the removal to the Rue Vivienne, Nicolas Clément worked at the classifying and cataloguing of 35,000 volumes. He distributed them into methodical classes, and devoted nine years—1675 to 1684—to his work. But this first unravelling was soon insufficient. Less than four years after, he commenced a new inventory in twenty-one volumes, which occupied thirty years, having been finished in the course of March, 1714. This time the numbers amounted to 43,000 printed volumes; his twenty-three principal divisions, containing all the letters of the alphabet, are very nearly preserved up to our day. In 1697 the question of publishing this enormous work was agitated, and on this point Clément had a curious correspondence with a learned Dane named Frederick Bostgaard; he also, in a celebrated pamphlet, *Idée d'une Nouvelle Manière de dresser le Catalogue d'une Bibliothèque*, indicated practical observations; he resolved this arduous question for important collections by difference of sizes; but his project was not executed, although favoured from the first by Abbé Bignon.

As the collection was not available for workers, the work of Clément had only a relative importance. A councillor of the Prince of Waldeck, a German of the name of Nemeitz, who travelled in France in the beginning of the eighteenth century, having seen it in the houses of the Rue Vivienne, says that the library occupied then twenty-six rooms and contained 75,000 volumes in all; it was shown voluntarily to strangers, but not to the public. Nemeitz gives some other curious particulars as to the libraries of Paris (*Séjour à Paris:* Leyde, 1727, 8vo).

The bank of Law, that had been lodged for some time in the Hotel de Nevers, alienated by the heirs of Mazarin, soon disappeared with the ruin of his system. As we have said above, Bignon appreciated the importance of the neglected palace for commodiously lodging the royal collections. This was in 1721. The collection was about to be subdivided into four sections, or, as they were then called in the administrative style, four distinct departments: manuscripts, printed books, titles, and engraved plates. The master of the library pressed the Regent to profit by the occasion, to which he agreed. In the month of September the removal commenced, and from the Rue Vivienne, the royal library, the first in the world and the most valuable, as Naudé says, entered the former palace of the Cardinal, which it was never to quit again.

We approach the epoch when this great scientific establishment was to quit its private character and to open its doors to the learned of all countries. In 1735 it was decided to print the catalogue of some divisions only: theology, canonical law, public law, and *belles lettres*. This resolution coincided precisely with the opening of the doors which took place in 1737, in which year appeared the first volume of the catalogue comprising the sacred Scriptures. At the end of the eighteenth century the royal library was finally established; the printed books then comprised about 200,000 volumes, and access was had by a staircase leading to six grand saloons, which were surrounded by galleries. From this moment the rooms became too small. At the Revolution the number of books had increased to 300,000, and projects of enlargement commenced, to be continued to our time; but, in spite of these proposals, the surface occupied by the library has remained the same since the time of Louis XV. Enlargements and alterations have been made year after year on the same ground without much new construction. But how the treasures have been augmented to this time! If the printed books at the Revolution represented a little more than 300,000 volumes, to-day they exceed two millions; the prints number two and a half millions; the medals, 100,000; the manuscripts, something over 90,000.

If we have thus brought the summary history of the National Library of Paris to our days, it was to avoid mixing it with other matters. We have entered into such detail regarding it as is fitting for the most important library in the world. We now return to the seventeenth century.

At the time when Henri IV. carried from Fontainebleau to Paris the nucleus of volumes that was to have so brilliant a destiny, the passion for books had singularly spread itself in France. We have already spoken of Mazarin; after him Cardinal Richelieu designed to open his private collection to the public, and in his will he manifested his clearly held intention. He went further in his last wishes: he prescribed the daily sweeping and dusting of the precious collection, and its augmentation by a thousand livres tournois each year. The great personages of the time were not behind; and Sauval says that in the seventeenth century there were 1,000 or 1,200 private libraries in Paris, numbering 1,700,000 volumes.

In the provinces there were few public libraries. The communities and learned Societies, the Jesuits and other religious houses, and the universities had collections At Orleans a library was opened for Germans, and the students of that country were able to work at their ease under the supervision of two librarians.

At the end of the eighteenth century the number of libraries had increased in large proportions; the amateurs had made their influence felt. The Book was not sought only for what it contained, but also for its exterior clothing. Only the great libraries open to everybody remained eclectic, and provided a little of everything. Besides the royal library, there were in Paris a great number of other collections, which the revolutionary storm upset and often destroyed. That of St. Germain des Près was burnt in 1794. That of St. Geneviève, founded in 1625, had benefited by celebrated donations, among others those of the cardinals De Berulle and De la Rochefoucauld; the Arsenal, created by the Marquis de Paulmy, was successively enriched by important acquisitions, among which was the collection of the Duc de la Vallière. These collections still exist, and are open to the public, as also are the National Library, the Mazarine, the Sorbonne, the Museum, the School of Fine Arts, the City of Paris, the Institute, the Louvre, and the several scientific faculties.

The provinces have not been behind in the movement. Many of the great cities contain a considerable number of books easily accessible, among them the libraries of Bordeaux and Rouen, amounting to 150,000 volumes; Troyes and Besançon, 100,000, etc. Few important centres have less than 20,000. These collections have been generally composed of those of the religious establishments, closed by the Revolution.

In our time public libraries are augmented by the legal deposit, gifts of the State, legacies of private persons, and purchases. The legal deposit in France relates almost exclusively to the National Library, and proceeds from the measures taken by Henri II. in 1556. Each French printer has now to deposit a certain number of copies of the works that he issues, and these volumes go to swell the number of books in the Rue de Richelieu. At the rate of 30,000 a year, the time is easily anticipated and very near when the space will be found insufficient. Some measures will have to be taken.

Germany, the cradle of printing, was not favoured in the beginning. It had, however, in the seventeenth century, in Wolfenbüttel, a little town in the duchy of Brunswick, a curious collection of books, in a detached building, of which the engraver Merian has preserved for us the physiognomy; it contained nearly 200,000 volumes, an enormous number for the time. The rather low rooms were shelved all round; in the middle were cases of the height of a man, also filled with books; the readers helped themselves, and were seated for working. The exterior of the building, without being sumptuous, was isolated and detached. In our time this collection includes the Bible, glass, and inkstand of Luther and his portrait by Lucas Cranach.

Another curious library, dating from the beginning of the seventeenth century, is that of the city of Leyden. An engraving by Woudan shows its state in 1610, with its classifications and divisions. The books were ranged in cases provided with breast-high desks. The books were placed with the edges in front, and not as now, and were so attached that they could only be consulted in their place. Each body of shelving contained a series of authors: theology, philosophy, mathematics, history, medicine, law, and literature. The room, of square shape, was lighted by windows right and left. Between the bays were portraits, views of cities, and maps. On the right, in a shrine, was enclosed the legacy of Joseph Scaliger. Communication was less liberal than at Wolfenbüttel; the readers were obliged to take the books from the shelves themselves and read them standing before the desks.

In England, the celebrated Oxford Library should be mentioned, augmented and restored in 1597 by Sir Thomas Bodley, ambassador of Queen Elizabeth. The generous overtures of this rich gentleman met with unanimous approbation. He offered to the library of the university the volumes collected by him during his travels on the Continent, whose value exceeded £10,000. The first stone of a new building was laid in 1610, but from 1602 the collection was open to readers in a provisional locality. David Loggan, the engraver, has preserved for us interior views of the Bodleian of the seventeenth century. The rooms are disposed in the form of the letter H, with pavilions to east and west, united by a gallery. The books were and are still in the body of the library, placed against the walls, with tables and immovable seats. The volumes were not displaced; they were consulted in their own place. Each room had two floors, with access to the second by stairs.

In London it was Hans Sloane who had the idea of founding a great collection by offering to the State for £20,000 his collection of books, which was valued at £50,000. Created in 1753 by an Act of Parliament, the British Museum, as it was named, was quickly augmented by many private libraries, among which was the library of printed books and manuscripts collected by the kings of England from Henry VII. to William III., which was added in the reign of George II. The very extensive and valuable library of George III., 250,000 volumes, was added by George IV. The Harleian collection added 7,500 volumes, and Robert Cotton his manuscripts. To-day the printed books amount to 1,300,000, and are only surpassed by the National Library of France as well in number of books as in number of readers. This immense collection increases at a great rate, one source being the compulsory deposit of a copy of every new book in order to secure copyright. Donations and legacies are constantly being made, and an annual sum for purchases is voted by Parliament. Besides the copy deposited by publishers in the British Museum, the law of copyright compels the deposit of four other copies, which go to augment the collections of the Bodleian Library of Oxford, the University Library of Cambridge, and the libraries of Edinburgh and Dublin.

If we search among the cities of Europe where establishments of this kind are most honoured, Berlin will take the third place with 900,000 printed books and 20,000 manuscripts, preserved in the Imperial Library. The building, constructed between 1775 and 1780, owes its special form to Frederick II., who desired that it should take the form of a chest of drawers. On the façade an inscription in the Latin tongue, but conceived in German spirit, indicates that here is a spiritual refectory—*nutrimentum spiritus*. Following come Munich, with 800,000 printed books; Vienna 400,000; Dresden, 300,000; then the universities: Leipzig, whose library, founded in 1409 and reorganised in 1830, contains 150,000 books and 2,000 manuscripts; Heidelberg; Göttingen, etc.

In Italy, Florence keeps, in the National Library, 300,000 volumes, proceeding from various amateurs, and formed since 1860. The collection of the goldsmith Magliabecchi, that was open to readers since 1747, has been transported there. Besides this library, Florence possesses the celebrated Laurentian, created by Cosmo de Medicis in the middle of the fifteenth century, where are united more than 8,000 manuscripts of an incalculable value. Milan has at the Brera a collection of 200,000 printed books and 50,000 medals, and at the Ambrosian, due to Cardinal Frederick Borromeo, 160,000 printed books and 8,000 manuscripts.

Rome possesses a dozen collections and celebrated deposits. The Vatican, not numerous, is most choice; the importance of its manuscripts is known to the entire world, but only a part of the 50,000 printed books are catalogued. The Library of Victor Emmanuel, formerly of the Jesuits, amounts to about 66,000 volumes. At Venice the splendid monument called the Antiqua Libraria di St. Marco has changed its destination; constructed in the sixteenth century and commenced by Sansovino for a library, it is now a royal palace. This city has lost that which had made its glory, and its collections are very modest in our days.

The magnificent educational establishments in the form of public libraries provided in the United States deserve special mention. Nearly every city has its public library, supported by a small tax; and many large libraries are wholly supported by private munificence. The first to be established was founded in 1732 by Benjamin Franklin in Philadelphia, and still exists as the Library Company; many important bequests have been made to it, the latest being £200,000 by Dr. Richard Rush. The library now numbers 150,000 volumes. The Congressional Library of Washington, besides its annual income from Government, receives by deposit for copyright a copy of every work published in the United States; it now has 565,000 volumes.

The Astor Library and the Lenox Library of New York were both founded and endowed by the families whose name they bear; the former has 223,284 volumes, the latter 25,000. The city of Chicago recently fell heir to the magnificent sum of over one million sterling for the establishment of a library of reference, and New York was benefited by the late Mr. Tilden to the extent of £800,000 for a public library.

When we have named the libraries of St. Petersburg and Moscow for Russia, Stockholm for Sweden, and the Escurial for Spain, we shall have mentioned very hastily the most important establishments in the world. For more than four centuries the love of books has preserved and fortified itself, and increases each day. If we were to endeavour to approximately imagine the number of printed books diffused, we should be frightened at it. It is by miles that to-day are counted the shelves of the National Library or of the British

Museum; and each year the production is accelerated, as is also the number of readers.

THE END.